John Hersey Revisited

Twayne's United States Authors Series

Warren French, Editor

University of Wales, Swansea

TUSAS 569

JOHN HERSEY
© *Rollie McKenna*

John Hersey Revisited

By David Sanders

Harvey Mudd College

Twayne Publishers
A Division of G. K. Hall & Co. • Boston

John Hersey Revisited
David Sanders

Copyright 1991 by G. K. Hall & Co.
All rights reserved.
Published by Twayne Publishers
A division of G. K. Hall & Co.
70 Lincoln Street
Boston, Massachusetts 02111

Copyediting supervised by Barbara Sutton.
Book production by Gabrielle B. McDonald.
Typeset in Garamond
by Compositors Corporation of Cedar Rapids, Iowa.

First published 1990.
10 9 8 7 6 5 4 3 2 1

The paper used in this publication meets the minimum requirements
of American National Standard for Information Sciences—Permanence
of Paper for Printed Library Materials, ANSI Z39.48-1984. ∞™

Printed and bound in the United States of America.

Library of Congress Cataloging-in-Publication Data

Sanders, David, 1926–
     John Hersey revisited / by David Sanders.
         p.   cm. — (Twayne's United States authors series ; TUSAS 569)
     Includes bibliographical references and index.
     ISBN 0-8057-7610-9 (alk. paper)
     1. Hersey, John, 1914–   —Criticism and interpretation.
 I. Title.   II. Series.
 PS3515.E7715Z88   1990
 813'52—DC20   90-41057
                                                               CIP

In memory of my mother and my father.

Contents

About the Author

David Sanders is professor of English at Harvey Mudd College, where he has been Miller Professor of Humanities, chairman of the Department of Humanities and Social Sciences, and chairman of the faculty. He has also taught at UCLA (where he received his B.A. in 1949 and Ph.D. in 1956) the Claremont Graduate School, the University of Maryland, and Clarkson University. He has been Fulbright lecturer at the University of Salamanca in Spain and visiting research professor at the Institute of American Studies, Academia Sinica, Taipei.

Sanders is the author of *Studies in "U.S.A."* and *John Dos Passos: A Comprehensive Bibliography*. His articles, reviews, and poems on various subjects have appeared in such publications as *American Quarterly, Lost Generation Journal, National Pastime, Paris Review, South Atlantic Quarterly, Spitball*, and *Studies in American Fiction*.

Preface

John Hersey was still teaching at Yale—the writing of fiction one semester, the application of fictional techniques to journalism the next—when he began work on *The Call,* a novel about a missionary in China. The hero would be his father's contemporary, starting out as a YMCA secretary in Shanghai in the first decade of the twentieth century, as Roscoe Hersey did in Tientsin, and his career would go beyond the elder Hersey's retirement to the virtual end of the Protestant mission in 1949. Although Hersey states that the fictional David Treadup is drawn from the lives of six actual missionaries, including Roscoe Hersey, it is obvious that he is more than this composite. When Treadup is interned by the Japanese in 1942, cut off from his work and despairing of his God, he becomes the central, even the culminating, figure for all of the contemporary history in Hersey's fiction and reportage.

Treadup is also a writer. His voice cries out from his diaries and letters so insistently that his obsession with his work and, even more, his self-centeredness must come from Hersey's knowledge of a novelist's life as much as anything the writer could have got from the papers of his six missionaries. The writing of *The Call* in the late seventies and early eighties coincided with Hersey's publishing a small flood of reminiscences. He remembered his first job with Sinclair Lewis and details of his longer employment by Henry Luce. In 1981 he went to his native Tientsin after an absence of thirty-five years—much of that time fearing he would never see China again—and wrote an account of the visit and the memories it evoked in a series for the *New Yorker.* When *The Call* was published in 1985, Hersey, who had interviewed Ralph Ellison and John Cheever, finally agreed to be interviewed himself. All of this helps to make *The Call* Hersey's most personal novel, his crowning work (as many have judged it), and the occasion for any of his longtime readers to reconsider his other writing.

My book on John Hersey for the Twayne United States Authors Series was written in 1965 after I had read *White Lotus,* an ambitious novel strangely savaged by many reviewers. I understood the story of American whites enslaved in a Chinese yellow empire as primarily a parallel to the history of African slaves and their descendants in the United States. While I realized that Hersey's childhood as a foreigner influenced this work, I could not have known then that it enabled him to imagine how this story might be told.

That is only one perception of Hersey's earlier work that came to me after reading *The Call* and then going back to Hersey's reports from China in the confused times of 1945 and 1946. *John Hersey Revisited* is as much a new reading of the work up to *White Lotus* as it is an introduction to what Hersey has written since.

Chapter 1 is about Hersey's career as a correspondent for *Time* and *Life; A Bell for Adano,* with its background in immediate events; and *Hiroshima,* which is partly shaped by what Hersey has called "the possibilities of fiction." Chapter 2 describes the writing of *The Wall* and how Hersey's obligation to tell of what he had seen and heard in Eastern Europe at the end of the war led to "Noach Levinson's archive," the strange form this massive novel assumed. Chapter 3 examines four novels from a decade that Hersey gave almost entirely to writing fiction. One of them, *A Single Pebble,* with its young American engineer hoping to transform China with his technology, can be read now as the beginning of a story that ends in *The Call.* Chapter 4 is devoted mostly to the narrator of *White Lotus,* whose singular language is Hersey's English "translation" of the Mandarin she acquired as a slave stripped of a very meager American culture. Chapter 5 considers the writing Hersey got done in twelve years as Master of Pierson College and adjunct professor of English at Yale: an investigation of the 1967 racial tensions in Detroit; novels and a polemic about education that derive from his concern with the fate of bright children in a democratic school system; and writing about writing in allegory, *Under the Eye of the Storm,* a historical novel, and commentary in *The Writer's Craft.* Chapter 6 is a reading of *The Call,* which carries over to a conclusion in which Hersey is discussed among his contemporaries as a distinguished novelist of ideas and a central figure for understanding differences between fiction and journalism.

I am grateful to Warren French for a discerning, meticulous reading of this manuscript and to Liz Traynor Fowler, Barbara Sutton, and Rob Winston for editorial assistance. Help from Murray Berman and the late Ted Weissbuch on my original *John Hersey* has been no less valuable for this book. I have remembered Sylvia Bowman's reading of that manuscript many times in writing this one. I thank Professor Tad Beckman, chairman, humanities and social sciences, Harvey Mudd College, for granting me travel funds, and Donna Schaefer and Fay Hicks for assistance with the laser printer. As always, Honnold and Sprague Libraries of the Claremont Colleges gave me invaluable support. In 1986 I spent a semester at the Institute of American Studies, Academia Sinica, Taipei, drawing a certain inspiration for this book, particularly from my good friend Chu Yen, dean of liberal arts at Taiwan National University, while I worked on other projects. That visit and a brief trip to the mainland stirred memories of China and the far Pacific as I had first known them more than forty years earlier.

I thank John and Barbara Hersey for their hospitality at Vineyard Haven, where I interviewed the writer for most of a brilliant day in view of the water. He has graciously answered my questions on many other occasions and sent me such elusive materials as "Intelligence, Choice, and Consent" and "The Need for Memory." I am grateful for his encouragement over the years and even more for having met him.

I have dedicated this book to my parents, remembering especially ten years of childhood in Peru, where my mother taught and my father was a metallurgical engineer, not a missionary. My daughter-in-law, Tracey Pera Sanders, found a way to get me started on my word processor, fitly enough on Thanksgiving weekend two years ago. All of her new in-laws help sustain me, now from many parts of this country, as they have before. I owe most to my wife, Mary-Frances, who was at Taipei and Vineyard Haven, as well as at Claremont and Lake Ozonia day by day, for the happy time of writing this book.

David Sanders

Harvey Mudd College

Chronology

1950   *The Wall*, April.

1953   *The Marmot Drive*, November. At thirty-nine, becomes the youngest writer ever elected to the American Academy of Arts and Letters.

1954   Member of National Citizens Committee for the Public Schools, the first of many activities on national and local levels of public education.

1956   *A Single Pebble*, June.

1956–1957   Visits relocation camps near the Austro-Hungarian border and writes continuity for a United Nations film on Hungarian refugees.

1959   *The War Lover*, September.

1960   *The Child Buyer*, September.

1963   *Here to Stay: Studies in Human Tenacity*, January.

1965   *White Lotus*, January; begins five-year term as Master of Pierson College, Yale University, 26 May; reads from *Hiroshima* at White House Arts Festival, 2 June.

1966   *Too Far to Walk*, February.

1967   *Under the Eye of the Storm*, March.

1968   *The Algiers Motel Incident*, June (report on 1967 riots in Detroit).

1970   *Letter to the Alumni*, September (report on events at Yale in the spring of 1970); on leave from Yale at the American Academy in Rome, 1970–71; adjunct professor of English at Yale until retirement in 1984.

1972   *The Conspiracy*, March.

1974   *My Petition for More Space*, September.

1975   *The President*, April (from *New York Times Magazine* article on President Gerald R. Ford).

1977   *The Walnut Door*, September.

1980   *Aspects of the Presidency*, June (republication of *The President* and 1951 *New Yorker* article on President Harry S. Truman).

1981   Visits Tientsin and other sites in China for the first time since 1946.

1985 *The Call,* May; new edition of *Hiroshima* with epilogue on fortieth anniversary of bombing, 6 August.

1987 *Blues,* May.

1988 Commentary for *Manzanar,* collection of Ansel Adams's photographs of Japanese American relocation in 1942.

1989 *Life Sketches,* June (essay collection).

1990 *Fling and Other Stories,* March.

Chapter One
Reporting Fact, Inventing Fiction

> I have always believed that the *devices* of fiction could serve journalism well
> and might even help it to aspire now and then to the level of art. But I have
> tried to honor the distinction between the two forms.
> —Hersey, "The Legend on the License" (1980)

For more than fifty years John Hersey has reported fact and invented fiction.
He has taken pains to draw the line between them, and he has been severely
tested in holding to that line. As he gained a reputation for reporting with
Into the Valley (1943) and dispatches for *Time* and *Life,* he became, very
suddenly, a best-selling novelist with *A Bell for Adano* (1944) and the incred-
ulous winner of the Pulitzer Prize for fiction on 8 May 1945—VE-day. His
wartime journalism—the articles based on observation in the field, not the
summaries of events he ground out in *Time*'s New York headquarters—bore
what Hersey later called "the legend on the license" of reporting: "NONE OF
THIS WAS MADE UP."[1] The wartime novel, on the other hand, *had* to be
made up, because he felt he could not merely report the story of General
Patton. Hersey invented a conflict between an arrogant, grandiose general
and a sensitive, pragmatic American military governor, and the resulting fiction became an earnest statement on the prospects for peace as well as the
conduct of war. Two years later he would interview survivors of the first
atomic bomb for an account of what he had not seen and could barely begin
to imagine. *Hiroshima,* touched with a novelist's technique, would be so
praised as journalism that it overshadowed not merely *A Bell for Adano* but,
for some critics, all of Hersey's subsequent efforts to write fiction.

Hersey's singular career began professionally when he reported to work for
Time in 1937, attracted by what he judged to be "the liveliest enterprise of its
type."[2] As with most other writers, signs of his vocation had come when he
was much younger, even as a missionary's youngest child in Tientsin, publishing "The Hersey Family News." Although his four years at Yale were also
filled with football and a combined major entitled "History, Arts, and Letters," it was there that he gave up the violin for writing. A year at Clare College, Cambridge, extended his idea of writing to include poetry and fiction.
At twenty-three, wanting to become a writer, he spent a summer in New

York City and Connecticut as secretary and general factotum to Sinclair
Lewis. Although Hersey was charmed by Lewis, he read the fresh typescript
of *The Prodigal Parents* and silently perceived its inferiority to the earlier
Lewis novels he had read.[3] The job at *Time* came from persistence and contacts, and Hersey became one of the anonymous young men writing "Mile-
stones" and "Miscellany." He gained no such reputation as James Agee's for
film reviews that needed no bylines, but among colleagues who also included
the poet and classicist Robert Fitzgerald, Hersey's style could often be identified in almost any section except "Science."

He went to work for Henry Luce a few weeks after Japanese troops had
stormed across the Marco Polo Bridge in Peking in July of 1937, the incident
most commonly marking the beginning of the Sino-Japanese conflict that
became subsumed in World War II. His career with Luce's publications was
affected considerably by the American "mishkid" background in China he
shared with Luce and by striking differences between Luce and Hersey missionary households. According to some accounts, the bond was once strong
enough for Luce to think of Hersey as a possible successor by the time he sent
him on a brief assignment to the Chungking bureau in 1939.[4] They did not
then disagree as implacably as they would later about virtually every Chinese
question except the imperative of victory over the Japanese. Filing his first
stories from overseas, Hersey had yet to earn a byline.

The peculiar anonymity *Time* imposed on its staff was one condition of a
news-gathering system that departed from the American journalistic
backgrounds of earlier writers. Ernest Hemingway, working with rewrite
men at the Kansas City *Star,* experienced something closer to *Time*'s pro-
cesses than anything such reporters as Stephen Crane and Walt Whitman
ever knew, but none of them—not even Hemingway dispatching cables in
the early twenties—undertook such labors of summary and reduction as
were routinely assigned to Hersey. John Reed and Richard Harding Davis
traveled far on assignments, but not so quickly or abruptly as Hersey did in
flying from one theater of World War II to another.

In their anonymous undertakings, Hersey and his colleagues were often
subject to Henry Luce's personal journalism, which may have reached an extreme with Whittaker Chambers's editing of foreign reports from Hersey
and others in 1944–45, but it was often expressed directly from Luce to a
writer. It grated more keenly on Hersey than on his colleagues because he
knew more about its source than they did. Roscoe Hersey, the reporter's father, was a YMCA secretary posted to Tientsin, while the publisher's father,
Henry Winters Luce, had gone out to China almost a generation earlier as a
Presbyterian missionary. The elder Hersey was influenced by the social gos-

pel, and most of his work was taken up with improving the quality of every-day life in China. The elder Luce, by contrast, was primarily an evangelist, even though (in Hersey's words) he was "destined to be not a soul-saver, but a fund-raiser."[5] The writer's Tientsin childhood, as he has described it, was spent in and out of the missionary household, roaming the city's nine foreign concessions. Hersey quotes Henry Luce saying of his Chefoo school days that Americans "were a strong, conspicuous, successful minority" at a place where "hardly an hour passed that an American did not have to run up the flag."[6]

In 1939 Hersey and Luce were nominally neutral Americans when the writer was sent out to *Time*'s Chungking bureau and traveled as well to Japan and to occupied China, including Tientsin. In Chungking, Hersey hired Theodore White as a stringer, beginning another *Time* and *Life* career that would crumble at the end of the war in disagreements with Luce over report-ing China's fate. White, then a recent Harvard graduate in Chinese studies, found in Hersey "every quality I then admired most in any contempo-rary. . . . Above all, he loved China . . . as much as I did or Luce did; and his fascination lay not so much with daily journalism as with history itself."[7] Hersey's love of China was then accompanied by a dislike, nurtured in child-hood, of Japan, an animosity he restrained during a quick stop in Tokyo to interview the American ambassador, Joseph C. Grew. In his first bylined arti-cle, Hersey noted that in the summer of 1940 "Japanese-American friend-ship [had] suddenly become a pressing matter."[8] The McCormick and Patterson newspapers were arguing for the practical necessity of a strong Japan, and numerous military experts, already focused on Europe, were ad-vancing the old maxim that it was better not to court trouble on two fronts. Ambassador Grew, Hersey wrote, was trying to prove a lifelong belief that "a gentleman can always get the better of a tough guy by continuing to act like a gentleman." Thus, a Hotchkiss and Yale graduate characterized a Grotonian and Harvard man. Grew frankly advocated befriending Japan, and, accord-ing to Hersey, he was remarkably successful: "After his complaints about the *Panay,* 70,000,000 Japanese considered themselves personally responsible to him." Grew practiced "dynamic appeasement," a strange phrase to come from the young correspondent who would soon be writing about "the Jap" in *Time*'s "World Battlefronts" department as well as in his own dispatches from the Pacific.

Hersey and others in the disastrous weeks after Pearl Harbor would grind dispatches from the Philippines and elsewhere into grave summaries running to four and five pages and appearing after "U.S. at War" and before "Foreign News." Candid about the unchecked progress of "the Japs" and limited by what the Allied military disclosed of the magnitude of defeat, "World Battlefronts" was an entirely typical reflection of contemporary anxiety. The same tone rings throughout Hersey's first book.

Eventually Hersey would persuade his publisher to delete *Men on Bataan* from the list of his published books. He disowned it, he said many years afterward, because it was "too adulatory of MacArthur."[9] It consists of alternating chapters about the general and the men under his command; the MacArthur sections form a brief biography going back to his boyhood at army posts, while those about his men are limited to the four months' action after 7 December. "You ought to know them for they are like you,"[10] Hersey wrote at the beginning of his first chapter on these men, using the direct address to readers that reinforced so much wartime journalism. Writing of MacArthur, he judged that it was important not to react too skeptically toward the MacArthur myths and proceeded to record how persistently the general was first and foremost in virtually everything he had undertaken. With little expressed reservation, Hersey quoted such MacArthur pronouncements as "By God, it was destiny that sent me here." It was equally difficult to avoid excessive praise elsewhere in the work, as when Hersey recounted Captain Colin Kelly's reported exploit of having sunk the Japanese battleship *Haruna* by crash-diving his fighter plane into one of its stacks. Indeed, Hersey committed every word of the book to the war effort, as when he assured his reader that his compatriots on Bataan had "reacted as you will when your crisis comes, splendidly and worthily, with no more mistakes than necessary." (7).

Hersey wrote the book in New York. It has in common with *Hiroshima* and *The Wall* Hersey's urgent effort—amounting to a duty—to report what he had not seen by a strenuously sympathetic effort to understand the testimony of those who had. In his circumstances in early 1942, he was understandably less resourceful and more limited in his means than he would be with his later books. He worked from *Time* and *Life* files, interviews with *Time* and *Life* reporters who had been on Bataan, letters from families of his servicemen subjects, and a Library of Congress bibliography of General MacArthur published in late February. MacArthur, ordered out on 22 February, left the Philippines on 11 March ("MacArthur's body was out, free and heroic. But his spirit was in the Philippines" ([310]); *Men on Bataan* was published in July. It may be remarkable that in the rush of putting the book together, Hersey would record some details of combat experience that he could verify once he took to the field himself. He wrote of Sergeant Joe Stanley Smith, one of the unlucky New Mexico National Guardsmen stationed on Bataan: "His sensations by his own account later took in everything from hot flashes to the calm a man feels only on the toilet seat" (22). This detail would anticipate what Hersey would learn on Guadalcanal, where he lacked the leisure to read the glowing notices of *Men on Bataan,* one of which might be chosen as particularly in keeping with the book and its time. In a special issue of the *Saturday Review of Literature* devoted to morale and edited by Eleanor Roosevelt, Fletcher Pratt wrote that Hersey's book "should be read by every participant in the struggle" and was "literature that will not be read with shame after the war." Someone at *Time* wrote slyly and anonymously that it was a book fit for a "hero-hungry United States."[11]

Into the Valley

Even as these reviews were being written, Hersey was on assignment in the Pacific. Aboard the aircraft carrier *Hornet* he interviewed Lieutenant A. W. Anderson, one of seven B-17 crewmen rescued from a four-man raft after they had crashed at sea returning from the Doolittle raid on Tokyo.[12] Hersey gathered his material in the carrier's sick bay, casting most of his dispatch in Anderson's words, with some information from other survivors. The piece was a step closer to writing about war he had observed firsthand, although it would prove eventually not to be the greatest influence upon Hersey from his *Hornet* experience. He also met the carrier's own pilots, not after they had been plucked from the ocean but after they had returned safely from one mission and were excitedly anticipating the next. They were not the subjects for an article, perhaps because the writer's stay on the carrier was so brief, and only part of his contact with them would appear in such later pieces for *Life* as "Experience by Battle," in which he stresses a distinction between Americans, who "love life so very much," even though they must kill, and Japanese, who kill under a code holding that "death is lighter than a feather."[13]

From life aboard the *Hornet* Hersey gained impressions that led much later to *The War Lover,* his novel of an American pilot who lusts to kill. Between his subsequent assignments to the Solomons and Sicily (which both led to books), he tried in "thirty to forty thousand words" to cast these imimpressions into a novella, "Sail Baker Dog," but dropped the project then, he has stated, because one of his models was offended by reading it.[14] He was also interrupted by the demands of events that brought more immediate challenges to his writing. Significantly, Hersey was attempting to write fiction almost as early as he was turning from *Time*'s overviews and rewrites to learn the techniques of writing about combat.

Barely five days before the *Hornet* was sunk, Hersey was sent to report the action on Guadalcanal in the Solomon Islands, where, after the Japanese had been stopped in the naval battles of the Coral Sea and Midway, an

American counteroffensive had begun with the capture of the Japanese air-field. History has confirmed the vivid expectation of the importance of the Solomons campaign and, perhaps, the difficulty of reporting the intensity and attrition of its daily skirmishes. There were at least two levels of such difficulty: one, the reporter's task of understanding all he could observe of combat in which his own life was at stake and two, writing accurately and thoroughly within censorship based on the premise that reporting was part of the war effort.[15] While no military censorship could be expected to uphold a writer's idea of truth against its own perception of military objectives, American reporters in the Solomons worked in an atmosphere influenced by efforts to conceal the magnitude of the disaster at Pearl Harbor. With his opportunity on Guadalcanal, Hersey was still burdened by anxieties that had governed the writing of *Men on Bataan*. Immediately after Pearl Harbor, he had tried to get into the navy but was persuaded by one of his editors to stay at *Time* on the ground that he would be more useful to the war effort there.[16] Those loyalties complicated his writing of "The Battle of the River," expanded later as *Into the Valley*.

On 8 October 1942 Hersey went with a company of marines into the third battle of the Matanikau River to force Japanese troops away from the sluggish stream, which was a natural defense line for Henderson Field. The first two battles, a frontal assault and an encircling maneuver, had failed because the attacking forces were too small. The third effort entailed a decoy holding attack at one point, another at the actual crossing point, and a third force behind these on the flank. Thus, Hersey was briefed by Colonels Simms and Edson before he went away with H Company under Captain Rigaud. "If I had had any understanding of what Company H might meet, I would never have gone along" (26), he wrote in 1942. Although a conventional enough tribute to combat marines, these words belie his obvious awareness of what he had learned and how much it meant to him. Intermittently under fire, at one point the company was pinned down by snipers and mortars as it was moving in single file. Later it was encircled, and a false order for withdrawal began to be passed back man to man along the line until it was stopped by the company commander. On the way out, Hersey saw a dead marine, whose "bitter young face said, as plainly as if he had shouted it, 'the Japs are bastards!' " (66). Shortly afterward he found a Japanese, stripped the dead man's helmet of its netting, and wondered who the owner might have been. It was a rare moment of wondering.

Hersey met the basic test of describing the physical hardships of the action: the heat, the chafing skin and aching muscle, the weight of a pack on his back, the whole contest between the jungle terrain and the human body from an intimate perspective he had not known on his earlier assignments. His own aches and pains helped him observe the greater suffering of the wounded and convey clearly the relative comfort of a marine with a severe shoulder wound beside the total indisposition of "Bauer" with a mortal abdominal wound. Hersey was one of "Bauer's" stretcher-bearers, on hand when he stirred to consciousness long enough to ask for help to defecate, and, having defecated, died. The accuracy of such detail is no more striking a sign of Hersey's growth as a reporter than his observations of the ordinariness of H Company's appearance, "men who did not look like people about to be offered up" and their "slight and fragile" leader, Captain Rigaud. Although the writer was still aware of censors reading his work as part of the war effort, he undercut fine phrases elsewhere in his account when he stated that the men were fighting "to get the goddam thing over and get home." They were "just American boys," volunteers, but were they, as volunteers for combat, inevitably "professional killers"? The question stirred Hersey to consider whether something in Rigaud's background had not determined what happened to the company "in the particular way it did." Rigaud had grown up an outdoorsman who also loved music and whose room caught the morning sun, and if such detail begins to imply the explanation Hersey sought, it shows that the reporter of "The Battle of the River" was closer to becoming a novelist when he rewrote his material as *Into the Valley.* Enforced leisure may have helped the process. Days after returning to marine headquarters from the Matanikau, Hersey was in two airplane crashes as he accompanied a crew on rescue operations. The second crash, a pontoon landing in the bush, laid him up for two weeks with broken ribs and delayed his moving on from the Solomons.

Hersey was on Guadalcanal little more than a month, much less time than most correspondents spent on such assignments, and so he wrote an account of a skirmish rather than such a record of sustained experience as Richard Tregaskis's *Guadalcanal Diary.* If Hersey lacked a veteran's awareness of any one campaign, he, perhaps more than any other American writer, was given a view of the full spectacle of World War II. From the Solomons he was sent to Sicily and subsequently to Russia. He reported land, sea, and air action; he interviewed men from each of the services, as well as civilian victims and returning veterans. He covered occupation, liberation, and rehabilitation. He encountered extreme censorship, both in the Pacific and in the Soviet Union, and, until past VJ-day, he was himself never entirely free of the viewpoint he had to assume in writing "World Battlefronts" for *Time.* These would be his advantages and limitations as a reporter before undertaking *Hiroshima,* and in 1944 they formed a curious background for a writer about to venture his first novel.

A Bell for Adano

While American forces were overrunning Sicily in July 1943, Hersey dropped by the office of the American military governor in Licata, a seaport on the southern coast, and worked his notes on the day's flow of visitors into an unpretentious dispatch that appeared a month later as "AMGOT at Work" in the back pages of *Life*. Meanwhile, the American military commander in Sicily, General George S. Patton, Jr., had entered Palermo victoriously and almost immediately afterward became the subject of shocking news stories. One recounted his slapping an American enlisted man and another his ordering a mule destroyed after its owner had failed to comply quickly enough with an order to get it off a road where it had been blocking military traffic. Hersey wrote nothing about these Patton incidents for *Time* or *Life* but in September took his considerable chagrin, along with his notes about the military governor at Licata, to Blowing Rock, North Carolina, where, "at white heat," he wrote *A Bell for Adano* in three weeks.[17]

Each person mentioned in the *Life* article became a character in the novel, and each problem dealt with by the actual military governor during Hersey's visit became an incident in the fictional Major Joppolo's career. In the day's proceedings at Licata, an eighty-two-year-old warns the Americans about the existence of a black market, a cart driver is brought to trial for impeding traffic and his case is dismissed, a wealthy householder is awarded damages for casual vandalism by American troops, and a pretty girl is told that her fiancé is alive as a prisoner of war. Most petitioners give absentminded Fascist salutes, and the military governor goes about his business as unassumingly as Sancho Panza dispensed justice on his island.

Hersey's General Marvin was based on Patton, often transparently, as in this hortatory flight from fiction:

> Probably you think of him as one of the heroes of the invasion . . . the man who still wears spurs even though he rides everywhere in an armored car. . . .
>
> You couldn't be blamed for having this picture. You can't get the truth except from the boys who have come home and finally limp out of the hospitals, and even then the truth is bent by their anger.
>
> But I can tell you perfectly calmly that General Marvin showed himself during the invasion to be a bad man, something worse than what our troops were trying to throw out. (47–48)

The bell of the title was entirely Hersey's own creation, his own symbol for the communal and fraternal spirit being restored by Joppolo's peace-building effort. Although Hersey has stated that writing this novel was the only way he could write what he felt about Patton,[18] the finished work shows that he was more inspired by what he had seen in Licata. *A Bell for Adano* is about hopes that come to the men and women who pick up the pieces the warriors leave behind. For all his savage obstinacy, General Marvin is only Major Joppolo's foil, and Hersey postpones his story of the war-lover type indefinitely to imagine instead a military governor's agenda that can represent the first tasks of the postwar world. Except for *Hiroshima, A Bell for Adano* has been Hersey's most widely read book. The struggle between the good Major Joppolo and the bad, or at least deranged, General Marvin is a vivid, uncomplicated story evoking the feeling of its time even after the Patton incidents have become misty in the general's later legend. The novel's immediate popularity was also due to widespread and often practical concerns about rebuilding the world after the war. In his study of Hersey's intellectual kinship with various contemporary thinkers, Samuel Girgus has shown that Hersey not only responded to the concerns but shared views on them with such advanced writers as James Burnham, author of *The Managerial Revolution*.[19] Hersey's novel also reads as a corrective, more than a fleshing out, of Henry Luce's hopes in "The American Century." In the foreboding winter of 1940–41, Luce had called for "America as the dynamic center of ever-widening spheres of enterprise, America as the training center of the skillful servants of mankind, America as the Good Samaritan, really believing again that it is more blessed to give than receive, and America as the powerhouse of the ideals of Freedom and Justice . . . a vision of the 20th Century to which we can and will devote ourselves in joy and gladness and vigor and enthusiasm."[20]

As their fathers had undertaken different missions in China, so in their wartime visions of peace is Hersey the reformer's son and Luce a second-generation evangelist. *A Bell for Adano*'s optimistic tone rises straight from the military governor's agenda Hersey describes in "AMGOT at Work": "Here at the major's desk you see difficulties, hundreds of them, but you see shrewd action, American idealism, and generosity bordering on sentimentality. . . . Above all, you see a thing succeeding and it looks like the future."[21]

Knopf published Hersey's first novel on 7 February 1944, and most reviewers praised it heartily. To Orville Prescott, Hersey exemplified a new breed of war novelist. Unlike some who had written about World War I, the writer could "look beyond both horrors and heroics and tell the truth to the best of [his] ability." Diana Trilling's review was a chilling exception to the run of tributes. Hersey's "ideas, like his prose, have undergone a conscious, falsifying, and purposeful simplification," Trilling wrote, implying that as a new novelist he was still a journalist recruited for the war effort.[22] While the judgment is mainly inaccurate and unfair, the reviewer may not have been able to overcome impressions of Hersey's intentions in his foreword (or of his even writing a foreword to a story told with such "simplification"). There the reader is bid to get to know Major Joppolo, much as readers of *Men of Bataan* were told that they should get to know each of the servicemen who were the subjects of that book's numerous anecdotes. (*"Therefore I beg you to get to know this man Joppolo well. We have need of him. He is our future in the world"* [vii].) Even this foreword, however, its prose redolent of radio scripts and advertisements of the time, reveals a point of view recurrent in Hersey's postwar thought when he states that the United States, in Europe to stay, with the invasion of Sicily, is more dependent on the actions of its Joppolos than in guidance from the Atlantic Charter or anything else *"so faultless on paper."* Readers who skip these opening italics start getting to know Joppolo as he steps ashore to make his first decision after the port is secured. Henceforth, the "Via of October Twenty-eight," named for Mussolini's birthdate, will be known as the "Via of July Ten," date of the American landings. The end of fascism is the beginning of some new system whose premises Joppolo will define with his work. Joppolo takes over the office of the *podestá* in Adano's *palazzo di cittá*, a cavernous setting that effectively suggests his immense and lonely task. On the way in, he has noticed the tower with its bell missing, presumably removed to be melted down for armament. The first live Italian to present himself to the governor begins to explain the bell's importance by detailing the townspeople's condition: they have been without bread for three days, the dead are unburied, the old authorities have fled, the water carts have not reached town in several days, no one believes in victory any more, and the bell is gone. He elaborates only on the bell. Everyone had lived by it. It was seven hundred years old and had rung in every hour of the townspeople's lives. Acting precisely as the man of wisdom Hersey has proclaimed him to be, the governor promises to replace the bell.

Whether Hersey "consciously simplified" his ideas is more arguable than the evidence that he was trying even more deliberately to tell his story simply. He established two deftly linked lines of narrative, one about Joppolo's efforts to find the right bell and the other tracing the major's conflict with General Marvin. After General Marvin has ordered the offending mule and cart destroyed at a crossroads outside Adano, he storms into the *palazzo di cittá* and, in Joppolo's absence, leaves an order prohibiting all carts from entering town. When Joppolo returns and learns that Adano's water supply depends on those carts, he countermands the order. Thereafter, the plot consists of Joppolo's efforts to get a bell in the tower before his countermanding order goes through the mazes of military routing to the general's desk. It was easy enough for Hersey (or any other war correspondent) to imagine sympathetic enlisted personnel all over the Mediterranean theater keeping the official papers bouncing around in courier's bags and lying at the bottom of the pile of documents on appropriate desks. For his Italian characters, Hersey had to draw from more than his recent notes on liberated Sicilians. In the fury of his writing, his great source was his memories of Chinese workers and peasants he had seen as he roamed through Tientsin and the countryside around the family's summer cottage at Peitaho, some of these memories recalling sharp assaults on his young conscience.[23] The most painful, to judge from its transmutation in the story, must have been of the day he accidentally tipped over a coolie's water cart while chinning himself on the edge of it to see what it held. As he recalled the experience in an interview more than forty years after he wrote *A Bell for Adano:* "The water spilled, and the coolie's labor of hauling it all the way there from the river was lost. He was not supposed to shout at a white child, but I understood why he did. His rage at me was something I have never forgotten."[24] This incident now casts its light into many corners of Hersey's long career, but nothing followed from it more directly than the pivotal incident of his first novel and his simple, compassionate treatment of the fictional cart driver's outrage. In the 1950s, Hersey was told by Carlo Levi, author of *Christ Stopped at Eboli,* that in Levi's own research for a sociological study he had found strong similarities between Italian and Chinese peasants. Hersey has repeatedly acknowledged Ignazio Silone as an early influence, but in 1987 he could not recall whether he had thought of either *Bread and Wine* or *Fontamara* while writing *A Bell for Adano* or whether when he read them he had been struck by the likeness of Silone's peasants to people he had known as a boy in China.

Hersey was awarded the Pulitzer Prize in fiction on 8 May 1945. The news reached him on a Manhattan tennis court, where his first thought was that his tennis partners were attempting a huge practical joke. Soon enough, though, he realized that the award was authentic, even if it was the most unexpected development in *A Bell for Adano*'s astonishing reception. The novel had been adapted as a play, and it enjoyed the great fortune of Fredric March's performance as Major Joppolo. It was being made into a motion picture; it had been condensed, serialized for the newspapers, and even translated for Soviet publication. Hersey had no illusions about all of this acclaim or that he had, as one critic judged, "everything needed to make a front-rank novelist."[25]

Some of this skepticism came from his assignment over the winter of

1944–45 to *Time*'s Moscow bureau, where he learned about the Red Army's triumphs, as all his Western colleagues did, by hearing the salvos fired in Red Square. He was more than compensated for this confinement when Soviet authorities took him on a tour well behind the advancing front to sites of German atrocities in Tallinn, Lodz, and Rodogoscz and to the ruins of the Warsaw ghetto. His reaction to what he saw was, of course, the beginning of the feelings and thoughts that led him to write *The Wall*. At the time, it was a revelation of the nature of this war that went far beyond anything imparted to him in the Pacific and Sicily, even beyond what he knew of Japanese actions in China. It may have supported his impression that winter that Soviet writers had been "in&out of the war" much more than he had. In a report on these Soviet colleagues published in *Time*'s book review section, Hersey said of their collective effort that "not a word is written which is not a weapon."[26] They limited their goals to a writing of such clarity and persuasion as would help defeat a hated enemy. Konstantin Simonov said so to Hersey directly, and the latter agreed that "the only fair test is to see whether [these] writers have fulfilled their aims." Writing later in 1945, Hersey doubted Simonov's claim that "people who can see what is happening around them, who can observe and assimilate events, have proved that it is precisely during the war and not after it that works universal in their bearing on life can be written."[27] Hersey found Simonov's *Days and Nights* inferior to passages he had just re-read in *Man's Fate, A Farewell to Arms,* and Mikhail Sholokhov's *And Quiet Flows the Don,* each written several years after the fighting it portrayed, although better than anything written by any American "I can think of who wrote during the war about the war."

While Hersey invites inclusion of *A Bell for Adano* and *Into the Valley* in that American war writing, he also reminds readers of burdens he shared with Simonov, both of them observers, both of them participants. In 1945, on the eve of departure for new assignments in the Far East, Hersey had a reasonably clear idea of what he had accomplished to that early point in his life as a journalist and a novelist. He also had daunting intimations of the writing that lay ahead of him.

Hiroshima

Hersey's greatest war reporting came after VJ-day in *Hiroshima,* a short account of the lives of six Hiroshima residents in the first hours and days after the first atomic bomb was dropped on their city. Factual yet imaginative, the book is so objective and impersonal that some readers have attacked it as an inappropriate response to the event. The reviewer for the *Times Literary Sup-*

plement wrote that it "spoke too quietly." Dwight Macdonald asserted vehemently that Hersey had no "feelings of intensity" and that "naturalism"— presumably Hersey's method, however understated—"is no longer adequate, either esthetically or morally, to cope with the modern horrors."[28] These have been decidedly minority opinions about *Hiroshima*. By the time a new edition, with an epilogue, "Aftermath," appeared in 1985 on the fortieth anniversary of the dropping of the bomb, sustained praise for the book had been followed by canonical statements that it was "the direct ancestor of the New Journalism" and an "exegetical nonfiction novel."[29] Aside from all such judgments, *Hiroshima* remains the piece of writing that, more than any other, made millions of readers attempt to imagine the actual details of the war's least imaginable military action.

Hersey went to China and Japan in September 1945 on assignment for both *Life* and the *New Yorker*. It was a stimulating time for him, even before he started to investigate the effects of the atomic bomb. Writing for both magazines, he was bound to neither as he had been to the Luce publications during the war, and he was also now free of military censorship. The result was a torrent of articles, most of them more discursive and speculative than his previous work, and even a few short stories. He returned to his native China at the beginning of the turbulence that preceded the long-threatened civil war between Communists and Nationalists and began filing stories for both magazines ("who intensely disliked each other")[30] about missionaries, American marines on duty and American sailors on liberty, and Chinese of several stations and conditions. Although Whittaker Chambers later accused him of being at this time among the Communist sympathizers at *Time* and *Life*,[31] Hersey was actually an apprehensive liberal in assessing postwar Chinese politics, and favored the "mild, gentle, rather frightened-looking, but really quite courageous" leaders of the doomed Democratic League.[32] Other subjects pushed him to levels of reporting and interpretation beyond his usual wartime work.

Try as he might to make sense of life in "Red Pepper Village" within the context of what he understood the world struggle to be, Hersey was resigned to recognizing the village's timeless routines. Unlike the cosmopolitan Tientsin of his childhood, this was a "China which goes on forever. . . , inhabits hundreds of thousands of places like Red Pepper Village, which absorbs its conquerors and plants its crops and pays no mind to political fashion."[33] Here he found people whose "horizon of understanding coincide [d] with the visual horizon," a thought-provoking coincidence for anyone outside such villages in 1945, let alone a writer graduated from the omniscient summaries of *Time*'s "World Battlefronts." Of course, he is describing a point of view like the one thrust upon the six survivors in *Hiroshima,* with the crucial difference being that their horizons of understanding had been much wider than the villagers' right up to the moment of the blinding flash.

"Two Weeks' Water Away," a report on the transporting of units of the Nationalist New Sixth Army from Shanghai to the North by American LSTs, reveals even more of Hersey's changing state of mind before he began work on *Hiroshima.*[34] He was aboard an LST whose commander strongly resembled the captain in *Mister Roberts,* petty, violent, and witless. The man had simple, emphatic views on China and American politics and was extremely wary of transporting dirty "Chinks" on his ship after several recent trips with comparatively clean "Japs." With most of the junior officers behaving as the captain did, Hersey drifted into conversations with the Chinese. Using the "practical Chinese" that came back to him from his childhood, he learned that several of them were from Tientsin and approached them almost as countrymen, "happier and straighter than people from Shanghai," until he was brought up short by a comment from a "Major Chow." "They're lazy," said the major. "They have no patience. They fight a lot. . . . But, on the whole the people of the North . . . all know how to suffer." Another American, "Lt. Jackson," assigned as liaison officer with the Chinese units, stood nearby, musing upon the ironies of a job for which he was unprepared through his total ignorance of the land, the people, and the language. "They laugh easier than any people I ever saw," he told Hersey, and then, after a few more comments, asked the writer, "Did anyone ever call you a *yang kwei tze?*" Hersey had indeed been called a white devil and, from early childhood, had been acutely aware of his foreignness, first in China and ever since in the United States. He would reflect upon it much more in his later novels set in China, but here, just before he went to Japan to interview people toward whom he had had deep antagonism, this was a sharp reminder of who he was. A towering white American foreigner in the land of his birth and never wholly assimilated into even the New York and New Haven enclaves of the land of his fathers, Hersey had developed a keener eye for the circumstances of other human beings than would be expected of a war correspondent on his abrupt arrivals and departures.

When Hersey and the *New Yorker*'s William Shawn first discussed the Hiroshima story, they planned to base it on the reporter's observations of the city's ruins, along with what he could learn of the actual bombing from survivors. While this plan might have produced a thoughtful article, Hersey, as an observer, was as distant from the real object of his curiosity as he had been from German atrocities the winter before when he was guided through the rubble of the Warsaw ghetto. While bedded down with the flu on a destroyer returning to Shanghai from North China, he happened upon Thornton Wilder's *The Bridge of San Luis Rey* and discovered a possible form for his article in the story of five strangers in colonial Peru thrown to their deaths when the rope cables snap on an ancient bridge over an Andean gorge.[35] Upon arriving in Japan, Hersey read both the *Report of the Commission on Hiroshima and Nagasaki* and the *Jesuit Report to the Holy See,* and to follow up on the latter was sent to the Jesuit mission in Tokyo, where he met a German Jesuit, Father Wilhelm Kleinsorge, and, through him, the Reverend Tanimoto, Miss Sasaki, and Dr. Sasaki, four of the persons who would be characters in *Hiroshima.* Hersey interviewed thirty men and women in all and chose six for his report. He used English in his interviews with Father Kleinsorge and the Reverend Tanimoto, and needed interpreters for the rest, thereby putting more distance between himself and the event or, when he was lucky, picking up some unexpected insight from an interpreter's tone or phrasing (a technique he refined in his research for *The Wall*). Hersey's distinctive understatement as the narrator was present from the earliest drafts, but its influence on the story has been exaggerated.[36] These are the survivors' accounts, not merely as told to the narrator but even more as he understands them. To express his own horror over the bombing or the plight of his interviewees, to be as overt and judgmental as he had been in his earlier books, would have weakened Hersey's effort to make readers understand what had happened. He was intrusive enough in selecting what he would use of each interview and much more so in shaping a single account from all the interviews. He interviewed his subjects before tape recorders existed, before any kind of recording device was standard equipment for investigative reporters, and therefore expanded and arranged his handwritten notes instead of editing and arranging taped interviews into a coherent report, as he would try to do twenty-two years later with *The Algiers Motel Incident.*

The first sentence of *Hiroshima* states where Toshiko Sasaki, a personnel clerk, was and what she was doing at the moment of the explosion at 8:15 A.M. on 6 August 1945. The second sentence is a cluster of such statements about each of the other five survivors Hersey chose to interview: Dr. Masakazu Fujii, operator of a private hospital; Hatsuyo Nakamura, a tailor's widow; Father Wilhelm Kleinsorge, a German Jesuit priest; Dr. Terufumo Sasaki, a surgeon; and the Reverend Kiyoshi Tanimoto, a Methodist minister. Only Dr. Sasaki was busy at work at that moment; the others, weary and troubled for various reasons, had paused then in their usual routines. The rest of the paragraph appears to stress their survival by "chance or volition"—

from the explosion that killed a hundred thousand other persons, some presumably no more vulnerable than they were. But the paragraph ends on another point: "At the time, none of them knew anything" (4). Inevitably, the account will be about how these six persons lived to tell their stories to Hersey and how they were brave or lucky as they left the destruction, but Hersey chooses to report less about the actions they take to survive than about their efforts to understand what has happened to them. Thus, Hersey exploits his own effort to understand—and the reader's.

At the moment of the explosion, all six survivors had been ill, tired, or worried for some time. They were not at their best when the "noiseless flash" happened, and Hersey notes, evenhandedly, the diarrhea or nightmare or fear of a B-29 raid on the strangely spared city that had possessed each of them. In the battered and xenophobic Japanese society of mid-1945, Father Kleinsorge suffered additionally from being a white foreigner and the Reverend Tanimoto from being a "security risk" who had learned his fluent English studying theology at Emory University. Hersey enters these background details briskly as the first chapter relates what happened to each of the six when the bomb hit:

It seemed a sheet of sun. . . . He [Tanimoto] felt a sudden pressure, and then splinters and pieces of boards and fragments of tile fell on him. He heard no roar. (8–9)

[T]he reflex of a mother set her [Mrs. Nakamura] in motion toward her children. She had taken one step . . . when something picked her up and she seemed to fly into the next room over the raised sleeping platform, pursued by parts of her house. (12–13)

Startled, he [Dr. Fujii] began to rise to his feet. . . . [T]he hospital leaned behind his rising and, with a terrible ripping noise, toppled into the river. The doctor, still in the act of getting to his feet, was thrown forward and around and over; he was buffeted and gripped; he lost track of everything because things were so speeded up. (13)

After the terrible flash—which . . . reminded him [Father Kleinsorge] of something he had read as a boy about a large meteor colliding with the earth—he had time . . . for one thought: a bomb has fallen on us. Then for a few seconds he went out of his mind. (18)

He [Dr. Sasaki] was one step beyond an open window when the light of the bomb was reflected, like a gigantic photographic flash, in the corridor. He ducked down and said to himself, as only a Japanese could, "Sasaki, *gambare!* Be brave!" (20)

Just as she [Miss Sasaki] turned her head away from the window, the room was filled with a blinding light. She was paralyzed by fear, fixed still in her chair for a long moment. Everything fell and [she] lost consciousness. . . . [T]he bookcases right of her swooped forward and the contents threw her down with her left leg horribly twisted and breaking beneath her. There, in the tin factory, in the first moment of the atomic age, a human being was crushed by books. (22–23)

Hersey does not attempt to account for what happened to his first five subjects beyond what they can recall, except perhaps in his generalization that "only a Japanese" would react as Dr. Sasaki had in telling himself to be brave. Whatever the accuracy of the remark, it was an odd yet unmistakable note of respect that dates the former war correspondent's peacetime assignment. Hersey had to account for how Miss Sasaki sustained her horrible injury after she lost consciousness, but the last sentence, so simply phrased, is his own open-ended irony.

The second section of *Hiroshima* is about the next few hours, as the great fire swept over the city. It begins with the Reverend Tanimoto, the interviewee who had the most comprehensive view of the damage. Having gone out to a suburb earlier that morning on an errand, he ran back in fear toward the center of town, hoping to find his wife. From his changing perspective of landscapes in fire and dust clouds, Hersey proceeds through the narrower awareness of the others, until reaching Miss Sasaki, as she regains consciousness in agony, alone and unheeded.

Hiroshima's readers, even the earliest, have known that the single atomic bomb dropped from the *Enola Gay* not only destroyed the city but left most survivors with unprecedented injuries and illnesses. Hersey's six interviewees have an immediate, tormented awareness of what they see, some making brief inferences of its meaning in the midst of more pressing actions. Some critics state that this knowledge withheld supplies the book's suspense,[37] but suspense is less compelling than the interest that develops from both the reader's sympathy for the victims and his curiosity over the appearance of details. Always stirred by the need to imagine what this experience was like, readers leap from one horrifying detail to the next, from one character to the next as each struggles with his instincts and his will. It was "incredibly fortunate" that the Reverend Tanimoto did find his wife running toward him as he neared the center of town, but their reunion is barely noted before Tanimoto is propelled into confused acts of mercy. Father Kleinsorge, whom the bomb had left in a stupor, became vaguely aware of his own cuts and bruises as he woke up to the suffering around him. Hearing the screams of people who wanted to be rescued, he somehow committed himself to saving Mr. Fukai, the Catholic mission secretary, who sobbed that he wanted to be left behind to die. After carrying Fukai several hundred feet, Father Kleinsorge stumbled, dropped him, and saw him run back toward the fire. The incident is a good illustration of how Hersey uses understatement. All that Fukai says is "Leave me here to die." Not even in Father Kleinsorge's immediate reaction to this request does Hersey permit any comment on this unyielding despair in the face of the general instinct for survival. Late in the next chapter Hersey ventures that Fukai may have sensed something final and hopeless about this bomb that set it apart from the firebombs that were desolating almost every other major Japanese city. Never, not even here, does Hersey state directly that Fukai was indeed the only person in his whole account who fled from the possibility of survival. In the summer of 1946, as the popular imagination described the advent of the nuclear age as either the beginning or the end, it was astonishing that Fukai's action was so underplayed.

The roaring wind flattened trees in Asano Park and brought large raindrops after the great fire. At this point, the reader will be jarred from the survivors' limited point of view to recall the phenomenon of "radiation sickness" and so break some of the spell Hersey has cast. One now anticipates this sickness striking each of the survivors, leaving them more exhausted than they had been during the numbing attrition of recent months. As the horrors increase, so does the pace of the survivors' efforts to save themselves and rescue others. The most appalling scenes are not so much understated as they are stated within the beleaguered consciousness of an observer. Father Kleinsorge, for example, stumbles upon a group of soldiers whose eyes had melted in their sockets (perhaps the single most horrifying scene in the book), but they are alive and thirsty and the priest makes a drinking straw of a thick grass blade so that they might draw water through the swollen apertures that had been their mouths. Meanwhile, the Reverend Tanimoto, having found his wife and left her in safety, makes his way back to his parsonage, where he sees a young woman, one of his parishioners, bent over the ground clutching her dead infant daughter. She would hold the dead infant this way for four days. When Tanimoto would return to her at intervals in his efforts to help others, he would try to persuade her to let go of the baby. Finally he began to stay away, but whenever he returned she stared at him and her eyes asked the same question, according to the account. Hersey's leaving the question unspoken and implying that he shares Tanimoto's awareness of what it was is an effective test of his method. To add his own indignation at that point would have dimmed the questioning eyes.

The third section continues to detail how each of the other four survivors existed within more restricted spaces and points of view: Dr. Sasaki, following an hour's nap after his first nineteen hours of dressing wounds, dragged back into a routine that was interrupted only by the news that someone had discovered exposed X-ray plates in the hospital cellar; Mrs. Nakamura, taken with her family into the chapel of the Jesuit novitiate; Miss Sasaki, being cared for after another two days and nights of lying alone in her agony; and Dr. Fujii, drinking whiskey, applying cold compresses to a broken collarbone, and mulling over the rumor that a fine magnesium powder had been sprayed over the city to explode when it came in contact with high-tension wires. A concurrent, less comprehensible rumor had it that "the city had been destroyed by the energy released when atoms were somehow split in two" (82). This hypothesis brought many readers in 1946 to the point where they had been the year before in assimilating early news stories. The third section concludes with the condition of the city as of 15 August, which Hersey does not bother to note as the day the Japanese surrendered unconditionally.

The last section of *Hiroshima* hurries from 15 August to Hersey's actual interviews. Aftereffects upon the six survivors varied in their manifestations, except that all six of them noted chronic fatigue, as though the weary, anxious state in which they happened to be the moment the bomb was dropped had lingered and got worse. Although they answered Hersey's questions willingly and were for various other reasons the six he chose out of thirty, we must assume that this fatigue affected their responses to any moral or theological issues raised by what they had endured. Some felt that there was nothing to be done about it (*shikata na gai*); Dr. Sasaki said that those who had decided to use the bomb should be tried in Tokyo along with others accused of war crimes. Hersey goes beyond his subjects' statements to cite the Jesuit report: "The crux of the matter is whether total war in its present form is justifiable, even when it serves a just purpose. Does it not have material and spiritual evil as its consequences which far exceed whatever good might result? When will our moralists give us a clear answer to this question?" (117–18). Many readers of *Hiroshima* have believed that Hersey offers such an answer with his account, thereby failing to hear him pose precisely the Jesuits' question. An honest liberal and a missionary's child who had lost his faith, he too was weighing the good and evil of the bomb's ending the war and was struggling for a clear answer.

Hiroshima's immediate public reception was unusual by any standards.[38] Albert Einstein was reported to have ordered a thousand copies and Bernard Baruch five hundred. The Book-of-the-Month Club sent free copies to its members because, its director said, the club found it "hard to conceive of anything being written that could be of more importance at this moment to the human race." Most American reviews were only a little less laudatory. *Hiroshima* was not read in Japan, where the American Occupational authority, which had been unable to ban pamphlets by Japanese nuclear physicists, prevented its distribution with stubborn effectiveness.

Replying to the Authors League in April 1948, General MacArthur's headquarters insisted that the book had not been banned, but when the League cabled back to learn whether this communication could be taken as authorization for the Japanese publication of *Hiroshima,* it received no answer.

Personal response to *Hiroshima* in letters, reviews, and public statements was intense in 1946 and has remained steady in the subsequent decades of nuclear weapons development. Nevertheless, the impact of the book has been questioned. In the most thorough study of its reception, Michael Yavenditti wrote that "Hersey's work aroused many readers but incited few of them. It enabled American readers to reaffirm their humane sentiments and to examine their consciences, but 'Hiroshima' did not require Americans to examine the legitimacy of the bomb's use."[39] There were in 1946, and there remain, two principal questions about the "legitimacy of the bomb's use": whether it should have been dropped on the Japanese cities and whether it should ever be dropped anywhere else. The first question poses a dilemma for anyone stirred alike by Hersey's report and by the prospect of the war with Japan having continued through an invasion of the home islands that would have entailed bombing all Japanese cities at the level of the B-29 raids on Tokyo. The second and greater question has been variously answered, always for the time being, through decades of confrontation that often broke into warfare; conscience, fear, calculation, and national interest, all fed by the imagination, have somehow kept the third bomb from being dropped. President Truman defended his decision tersely by inviting doubters to ask "any young man who was over there and see what he thinks about it." His chief of staff, Admiral Leahy, would write that "in being the first to use it we adopted the ethical standards common to barbarians in the dark ages."[40] Hersey, like many other young men who had been "over there," has been less certain than either the president or the admiral about the legitimacy of using the Hiroshima and Nagasaki bombs.

"The Aftermath" appears as the epilogue to a new edition of *Hiroshima,* published in 1985 on the fortieth anniversary of the Hiroshima bombing.[41] Hersey describes the later lives of his six interviewees, now *hibakusha* ("explosion-affected persons" rather than "survivors," because the latter term "might suggest some slight to the sacred dead" [120]), building upon a dominant theme for each person until he chooses to cast the Reverend Tanimoto's story within an outline of the postwar growth of nuclear weapons. Mrs. Nakamura worked so hard (and had to rest so frequently from her exertions) that "she had no time for attitudinizing about the bomb or anything else." (121) Dr. Sasaki also worked hard, "enclosed in the present tense" and eventually becoming a wealthy doctor who in forty years had never spoken about the immediate hours and days after the explosion. Father Kleinsorge became a naturalized Japanese and took the name Takakura; a victim of severe radiation sickness, he suffered lingering and variously manifested "debilitation" until his death in 1977. Miss Sasaki recovered enough from her hideous injury to become a Catholic convert, then a nun, known for "her ability to help people die in peace." Dr. Fujii, the bon vivant, accompanied the "Hiroshima Maidens" to the United States and observed the operations on their faces, cheering them while "having a wonderful time" himself. In 1963, after a household accident or possible suicide attempt, he became a helpless invalid for the remaining nine years of his life.

The Reverend Tanimoto, the Emory University graduate, devoted himself to peace movements and for many years moved about in Japan and the United States at a pace reminiscent of his hours of rescue work on 6 August 1945. Hersey takes two paragraphs to remind his readers of the earlier activity—a backward glance not given his other subjects—and begins a parallel that makes Tanimoto's frantic day after "the noiseless flash" a metaphor for the postwar search for peace. Tanimoto's work to rebuild his church led him in 1948 to write an Emory classmate, who promptly invited him to the United States to raise money. On the sea voyage over, Tanimoto was seized by a plan to establish a peace center in Hiroshima because "the collective memory of the hibakusha would be a potent force for peace in the world." By early 1949, he had preached "The Faith That Grew Out of the Ashes" many times and had shown his proposal for the peace center to Pearl Buck, who in turn had him send it to Norman Cousins, then editor of the *Saturday Review of Literature*. Tanimoto's proposal appeared in the 5 March issue as "Hiroshima's Idea," but, Hersey states, "the people of Hiroshima were in fact, to a man, totally unaware of Kiyoshi Tanimoto's (now Norman Cousins') proposal." For five years Tanimoto rode a roller coaster of celebrity and rejection. Local officials in Hiroshima refused to support him, for fear of offending American authorities (whose ban on disseminating reports on Hiroshima and Nagasaki bombing effects had already touched Hersey's article). On a trip to the United States, Tanimoto gave the opening prayer before a session of the Senate and months later was the stunned subject of a "This Is Your Life" television program, where the rapid-fire sketch of his life included a guest appearance by the copilot of the *Enola Gay*.

The Reverend Tanimoto missed forming early connections with the more effective Japanese peace movements and finally even lost touch with groups like the Hiroshima Maidens that he had helped to organize. Hersey states, with rare animosity, that "he had been hurled along on the whitewater of

Norman Cousins' ferocious energy." By implication, the actual and potential efforts of the *hibakusha* had become engulfed by American grandiosity at the very time—roughly 1950 to 1955—when they might have influenced a Japanese peace movement that was becoming increasingly political.

"Aftermath"—especially bound with the original chapters of *Hiroshima*—is a sobering, often bitter assessment of the impact the bombings have had on the world's conscience over forty years. Hersey suggests that whatever we learned then is indistinct now, that negotiation toward nuclear weapons limitations, let alone disarmament, has no clear connection with the first bomb and bears no demonstrable trace of the peace efforts of the *hibakusha*. In fact, Hersey almost ignores disarmament efforts in "Aftermath," punctuating his essay with an out-line of events that begins with the Bikini tests in 1946 and ends with India's first nuclear explosion in 1974. The exhaustion of the interviewees as they stirred about in the early morning of 6 August 1945 is perpetuated in the weariness of the *hibakusha*. Even Tanimoto slows down. "His memory, like the world's, was getting spotty" (196), Hersey observes.

Chapter Two
The Wall: A Novel of Contemporary History

We were all talking about one question: What has made our lives worth living?

—Noach Levinson in *The Wall (681)*

Seeing Hiroshima, Hersey has said, "lent urgency" to his plan of writing a novel about the Warsaw ghetto uprising in 1943.[1] This urgency overrode a host of inhibitions. Hersey was not Jewish, he had lost no one to what would later be called the Holocaust, he had no Yiddish or Polish for reading primary materials, and he had only a missionary child's exposure to the Old Testament to help him begin understanding the culture of European Jews. With very few distractions, he devoted himself for three years after *Hiroshima* to the research and writing of the long novel published as *The Wall* in 1950. It is the story of the Warsaw ghetto from its walling-in in late 1939 to the survivors' escape in the uprising. It focuses on a few families and is told with many digressions into an "archive" of the ghetto's culture. If it is not Hersey's greatest accomplishment, it is, beyond question, his most ambitious undertaking until the exploration of his own past that resulted in *The Call* in 1985.

Hersey has written two extensive statements about his work on this novel: in 1952, when he presented the manuscript to Yale University, and in 1984 for an address in Baltimore on "The Need for Memory." Both papers describe roughly the same procedures: the reading, the translators, the decision—almost at the end of the first draft—to abandon a third-person narration for a more authoritative voice, and the impetus this decision gave to the writing and rewriting that followed. In 1984, Hersey was more detailed about his inspiration from the wartime tour of Warsaw, Lodz, Rodogozcz, and Klooga, citing Bernard Weintraub (subject of his *Life* article "Prisoner 339 Klooga") and identifying Emmanuel Ringelblum as a Warsaw ghetto resident who had compiled an archive. But the great difference between Hersey's two papers thirty-two years apart is apparent when he writes in "The Need for Memory": "Now, there came with the years to be one man who was to be a conscience for all of us with respect to the Holocaust, named Elie Wiesel. He has raised disturbing questions. Had any writer who had not himself experienced the sufferings of that time the right to try even to imagine what they were like? Was such imagination even possible? Could there be any vision of those experiences outside of actual memory? Could even those who remembered convey the truth?"[2] Perhaps the burden of Hersey's self-examination is that the questions, in whatever inchoate form, haunted him the deeper he got into his project and led him to the final shape of his book.

As a correspondent in Moscow, he was taken in late September 1944 to the recently overrun village of Klooga in Estonia, site of a camp where the Germans tried to kill all their prisoners before retreating. There, in "an encounter that changed my life," Hersey met Benjamin Weintraub, who proceeded to tell his story at length shortly after Hersey had seen bodies still on the platforms that the prisoners themselves had been ordered to build. This was Hersey's first intimation of the extent to which the Germans had planned to exterminate European Jews. Four months later, the Soviets took him to see Lodz, the warehouse-dungeon at Rodogozcz, and Warsaw, where he stood beside the rubble of the ghetto. In 1984 he wrote of the magnitude of the revelation: "I did not know; we did not know." Noting the publication of *The Black Book of the Polish Jewry* in New York a year before he saw Klooga, Hersey added, "I could have known."

Early in 1947, conversations with an Auschwitz survivor deterred Hersey from setting his novel in the concentration camps.[3] He decided instead to go back to the survivors of the ghettos because they had lived as families and communities to the end. "Because of its legendary quality" that preceded even the uprising, he chose the Warsaw ghetto and began to read. He soon discovered an abundance of documentary material, all of it in Yiddish and Polish and unlikely ever to be translated into English. (He had been reading *The Black Book of the Polish Jewry* and other sources available in English.) He was lucky enough at that point to find a highly competent translator in each language[4] and, after several experiments in other means of transcription, had them read directly from the original text onto a wire recorder in rapid and "intensely moving" English.

Then Hersey lived with the recordings, which he "did not see as documentary" but "heard as felt experience." For months on end, listening to his translators, he found his approach to the novel changing mysteriously. The translators would skip or summarize and interject, becoming storytellers themselves instead of simply transcribers. They were shaping his decision to tell the story as several first-person narratives, from points of view of ghetto residents. The translators influenced him as he read I. L. Peretz, Sholem

Aleichem, and the Old Testament. One translator had lost his mother in the ghetto; the other, her brother-in-law. Their transcriptions made up about half of the two million words that went into Hersey's notes and records before he had completed researching *The Wall*. It was then late 1948, and he was still not ready to write.

He took notes on his notes, "as if I were interviewing the three of us—the two translators and myself." At times in the course of his preparations he had been tempted to seek out actual ghetto survivors but decided that he should get no closer than the transcriptions of his translators, which were compelling enough but still allowed him to create his own ghetto characters. He wrote a chronology of ghetto events, a list of fifty persons in the ghetto whom he thought he would like to know, and nineteen themes to appear in the book ("I. In danger, some men surprised into heroism; others amazed to find themselves corrupt. . . . V. Satisfactions in the company of death: intellectual activities, companionship, resistance, dreams of the future, and work. . . . XVIII. The wall").

He began to invent episodes, attaching characters and themes to them. Certain characters were beginning to stick out; among them, Noach Levinson changed from a Judenrat official to "a kind of intuitive historian." He was aware that such a man, Emmanuel Ringelblum, had existed but knew virtually nothing more of Ringelblum's career until years after *The Wall* was published. In Hersey's planning in 1948, the "intuitive historian" would appear as a choral voice between chapters of a narrative still set to be told in the third person.

Writing proved disillusioning. "What I wrote down fell far short of what I had dreamed, and each day's stint was poetry unrealized, unachieved," he said in 1952. Unconvinced by what he had written, he stayed with his long-hand draft until, four-fifths of the way through it, Levinson became too insistent. His choruses were now too long to stick conveniently between chapters, and Hersey was aware that he would have to begin the next draft at once. Levinson—and the storytellers on the wire recorder—had won out, and the archivist would henceforth be the person through whom the story would be told, whether through his comments now in the foreground or as the gatherer of all the other first-person narratives. In 1952 Hersey recalled this staggering decision almost playfully. "This particular story needed to be told with an authority my gifts could not evoke," he wrote in "The Mechanics of a Novel"; "it needed to be told by a participant in the events; and my creature, Levinson, some of whose literary mannerisms, I confess, were annoying, did seem to me to have the gifts, the background, and above all the experience to make his story believed."

His recollection thirty-two years later bears a heavier burden of reflection:

The real trouble, I finally realized, lay in the fictional point of view I had adopted. This story could not be told by an all-knowing, all-seeing John Hersey. There was a fatal falsity in the universal point of view in my hands. This story had to be told by a Jew. This story had to be told by a person who was *there,* by one who would, one day, become a survivor. In other words, I was confronted, long before a single word written by Elie Wiesel had entered my consciousness, by the essential difficulty he would lay before us all. Imagination would not serve; only memory would serve. To salvage anything that would be worthy of the subject, I had to invent a memory.[5]

Hersey went much faster on this Levinson draft. As before, he charted scenes and characters, observing that the second chart "looked like a purposeful graph. . . . I could see from the bare symbols the possibility of growth, change, and rhythm in the characters." Above all, Levinson took over. He spoke for the novelist who was reluctantly yielding authority and for the reporter who had not been there. And then the archivist became a character in his own right and ran away with something in the inner process of putting this sprawling novel together.

Levinson is introduced as the compiler of an archive—four million pages in minute Yiddish script about almost every phase of life in the Warsaw ghetto. (The millions of words of documents read by Hersey's translators had been written by many hands.) Levinson is contrived as the sole source of all that could be known about the ghetto, the sole transcriber of Judenrat business and of songs and plays; on the bedrock of his own intense comments, he is also the single tireless recorder of everything seen or remembered by his friends that might contribute some meaning to his project. If this heroic effort and forethought strains belief, Hersey at least gives Levinson his "invented memory," a lifelong vocation of remembering. Long before the Germans began to wall in the Warsaw Jews, Levinson had been taking notes, from personal observations, toward a description of Jewish culture, and, before starting this task in 1935, he had published two books, *The Diaspora* and *Customs.*

Levinson has conspicuous oddities and weaknesses to go along with his scholarly resolution. He is small and ugly, uncertain of himself in important personal situations outside his vocation, a lonely man who becomes a member of a family in the ghetto's worst hours. The reader might expect a gossipy curiosity from the stream of reflections Levinson showers on his friends' lives; it is more surprising to see him rise as one of the characters he records with insatiable industry.

Levinson is a true scholar. His method is impeccable and his curiosity unlimited. Each of several episodes begins with the formal notation "EVENTS JULY, 1942. ENTRY JULY 12, 1942. N. L." He gives reasons for every break in chronology, whether in events themselves or in his telling of them. Something that he may have transcribed without comment about one of his friends in a given entry is suddenly followed by his confession of having misunderstood that person. Levinson on occasion is his own gloss, much in the manner that Hersey had intended to offer comments in interchapters. Yet each gloss—indeed, the persistence of scholarly habit right up to the departure from the ghetto, a moment in which the scholar makes unexpected self-discoveries—helps make Hersey's complicated characterization believable. Although Hersey has always hailed Levinson as a fortunate invention, the new point of view had its own subtle problems. Levinson must not permit his self-characterization to restrict the independent development of such major characters as Rachel Apt and Dolek Berson; they cannot be merely figures he has observed. Going a step further, the reader must accept the condition that from archive entries he will gain Dolek's or Rachel's true opinions of Levinson. At times, the archivist is given a novelist's imagination to complement a reporter's skills.

Finally, from the volumes of his miscellaneous entries, Levinson is also responsible for the stories that exemplify Hersey's nineteen themes, all in some meaningful arrangement without imposing a didactic burden on the narrative. Nancy Lyman Huse is right to conclude that "a rather minute awareness [of Levinson] is the key to Hersey's purpose and accomplishments."[6] Such awareness demands that we notice the "Editor," as well. After accounting for the existence of the archive in a prefatory note, the "Editor" appears only in a few bracketed remarks that are models of impersonal comment. Ostensibly, he cuts and pastes from Levinson's materials, which Hersey, before assuming the fiction of his editorship, has, on the copyright page, called a "hoax."

The Wall is, obviously, more than its enabling device of the Levinson archive. It is a long novel about the Warsaw ghetto from November 1939, when German restrictions on Jews began to be enforced, to May 1943, when the last buildings were razed. It is Hersey's definitive example of what he described elsewhere as a "novel of contemporary history," fiction whose subject he saw as confusion in the history through which his readers had lived. Its attraction for the writer is obvious when he states: "Fiction can deal with confusion, but a journalist is not allowed to be confused; he must *know*."[7] In his first novel of contemporary history, Hersey has gone beyond the verified observations in his reporter's notes on the military government in Sicily to speculate about the foundations of peace in the postwar world. *The Wall* required of him the much greater effort of proceeding from the bewildering revelations thrust upon the reporter in the Soviet press tour of apparent atrocity sites in 1945. The novel's imagined history of the Warsaw ghetto—its confusion along with its heroism—became Hersey's greatest venture into the meaning of the war he had himself somehow survived.

The Wall is the story of a "family" of Jews from many backgrounds who depend on one another as their will to live grows along with the prospect of their certain annihilation. This contest is complicated because, as Samuel Girgus has observed, the Jews themselves have built walls and, to a lesser degree, because the Germans proceed toward their objective through a protracted series of decrees and harassments.[8] The will to live is expressed by some Jews as a determination to fight, by others in the deviousness of their accommodation to circumstances, and by a few in their denial of the possibility of being killed. For those who will fight, the will to live will also require the definition of a new way of life, because as the Warsaw Jews become more walled in, they lose the submissiveness and withdrawal into empty custom that characterized their earlier lives in unwalled ghettos. "What is Jewishness?" Levinson asks his friends in a lecture on his beloved Peretz. Light flickers and goes out in the darkened bunker, but the packed gathering "seemed, indeed, to be in a universal place, not limited by a wall, not bounded by fear and stench." Levinson draws Peretz's words from memory:

Now I am not advocating that we shut ourselves up in a spiritual ghetto. On the contrary, we should get out of such a ghetto. But we should get out as Jews, with our own spiritual treasures. We should interchange, give and take, but not beg.

Ghetto is impotence. Cultural cross-fertilization is the only possibility for human development. Humanity must be the synthesis, the sum, the quintessence of all national cultural forms and philosophies. (550)

This incident is the climax to the story of Levinson's career as archivist of Jewish culture, if not the climax of *The Wall.*

The novel begins with Levinson's first impressions of Dolek Berson, a drifter who loves to argue, during their imprisonment as hostages along with other members of the hastily recruited Judenrat. This first taste of the German occupation seems to be something they can deal with, despite what they have heard of Nazi racial decrees. Pavel Menkes, the baker, has told Berson that he will fight: "Overt opposition. Kill the rats. Show a fist." But whom would he fight, Berson asks, "Hitler in person? Rosenberg? The S.S. Commander for the Warsaw district? Or some individual German citizen complying, shaking his head but complying. Or, more availably, a Polish citizen, who didn't seem to need the decrees in the first place. Whom would this baker fight? . . . No . . . there is only one resistance: it is inward. It is living one's Jewishness as well as possible, meeting things as they come" (17–18).

Both Berson and Menkes are eventually proved correct when Jewishness becomes Resistance, but there are many other reactions at the inception of German rule. Jews of every conceivable background are driven into the ghetto and scurry about for situations. There are Zionists, almost jubilant with this justification for their militancy; Socialists, who cling to the idea of a working-class party linked to Socialists outside the walls; and Communists, who are utterly bewildered, given the impossibility, in that place and time, of rationalizing Soviet policy in the autumn of 1939. More obvious than these partisans are the *kinds* of people forced, some for the first time, to think of themselves as Jews. Some still call the ghetto's Sienna Street "the best kind of neighborhood" or believe, as Pan Apt does, that "money would do everything." Others, such as Rachel Apt, "memorize the Polish parts of their lives" when they begin living as Jews. Levinson observes that these people the Germans have blocked off as Jews are "a small France" in their divisions and distinctions.

The community begins to unify by resisting the Germans, whether by the Judenrat's evasions or in plans for eventually fighting block by block, house by house. Their children's schooling becomes a form of resistance, as do the religious services now conducted in their homes. But in all these activities of the early months, the Jews have been able to ignore the extremity of their plight. Only as the Germans post racial decrees, only as Pan Apt finds that money cannot buy his deliverance, and only as German soldiers form cordons at every ghetto exit do the Jews realize that they are locked inside their wall under circumstances that differ from any they have known.

The remaining five sections of *The Wall* are organized on parallel lines of development: first, in the progress of concentrated refugees toward becoming a compact group of fighters as their numbers dwindle and their territory contracts block by block; second, in the growth of a family, as such solitaries as Levinson, Berson, and Rachel develop intense loyalties to one another. The novel moves in as many short episodes as can readily simulate the archive, with Levinson's point of view dominant but by no means the only significant one. Levinson (like Hersey) not only asks questions but listens—sometimes so intent on word and gesture that he misses tones the reader can detect. Thus, the reader may recognize Berson's true capacities long before Levinson has stopped thinking of him as a charming drifter.

Levinson is not himself committed from the beginning to a plot line for his materials. He has been a member of an ancient literary tradition of patient accretion and limitless curiosity. Accordingly, in *The Wall* one is far less aware of a chain of circumstances than of a vivid collection of people, each caught up in actions that reveal the diversity of Jewishness as they are bound further in confinement. Levinson, for obvious reasons, and Dolek and Rachel, because they survive to escape, are the most important of these characters, but at least fifty others are as memorable.

There is wizened Fischel Schpundt, who makes the Germans laugh at him as he ridicules them. Rachel Apt's prettier sister, Halinka, seems to wither in her new surroundings until she captures a Zionist leader and undertakes her own dangerous missions for the Resistance. The old Socialist, Henryk Rapaport, never quite accepts the fact that his Polish comrades have little concern for his welfare. Young Schlome Mazur dies as he had lived, oblivious to anything outside his books, the least touched of anyone by the persecutions. Mordecai Apt typifies the intellectuals-turned-laborers (like Benjamin Weintraub, Hersey's interviewee at Klooga), grimly happy that they are at last being "brutalized for Jewishness." Wladislaw Jablonski, in the ghetto for his fraction of Jewish ancestry, poses as a Pole for years after he had been immured; his son, who "must have been asked questions," is happy to be known as a Jew. Stefan Mazur works as policeman for the German *ordnungsdienst,* filling up "resettlement quotas"; with more vexation than sorrow, he ponders sending his mother or his mother-in-law to the *umschlagplatz* for deportation. Fein, an authentic laborer, instructs the Bersons and the Apts in the use and care of tools so that they will not be hauled away as masquerading scholars and piano players at the next resettlement muster. Nameless figures are vivid, as when Levinson reports on a day at the *umschlagplatz:* "One little man, stripped to the waist, was flexing his muscles before a Junak and wrestling furiously with some water pipes against a wall to show how strong he was and what a mistake it would be to deport him. A young man, who must have belonged to some underground group, shouted: *Fools! You are being taken to death!* A woman spat on him and said contemptuously: *Troublemaker!*" (350).

Most of these people demonstrate that *The Wall,* despite all the suffering it describes, was inspired by what Hersey called "the defiantly civilized and most amazing flash of humane light, the ghetto uprising."[9] The novel ends not with the destruction of the ghetto, which the escaping Jews scarcely acknowledge, but with the escape of forty-two men, women, and children; forty-one finally, since Berson, at the rear guard pushing more exhausted persons up through the manhole to the street, is left behind when the trucks are spotted by the police. While the group had waited unexpectedly a day and a night in the sewers for the delayed trucks, Levinson ceaselessly interviewed his friends. According to Rachel, he *entertained* them:

RACHEL: It is strange. With Dolek, I have never been self-conscious about my face.

N. L.:   Perhaps your Berson is one of those men who never lets himself have a chance to look at a woman's face. Other interesting features . . . (626)

I reminded Rachel that when she first moved into the Jewish section with her family she had had very little experience of inner Jewish life. I asked her to tell me what she thought of this inner life, now that she was on the point of graduating from ghetto-school.

RACHEL: —I didn't have as much chance to learn about God; I am rather unclear as to God. But so far as the rest of our religion is concerned, I think there is only one thing: not to hurt anybody. For me the whole Torah is in one sentence in Leviticus: Thou shalt love thy neighbor as thyself. (627–28)

One must love one's neighbor, Rachel persists, even when that neighbor is a Nazi, because Rachel is now turned to the wholly new life to begin after the escape. It is she who is given the last words in the novel, spoken within Levinson's hearing as he pauses in the Lomianka Forest to pluck a leaf from a bush: "*Nu,* what is the plan for tomorrow?" This line concentrates Hersey's unflagging interest in what people will do once they have chosen to fight the prospect of certain annihilation. Lacking the authority of existential writers who had lived in occupied Europe, he nevertheless understood bare existence to the limit of his experience as a reporter, an understanding that impelled his imagination as a novelist. Much of what David Daiches called "the miracle of compassion"[10] in *The Wall* could be explained by Hersey's intense interest in the conditions and quality of survival. He had known people who drew life from the menace of death. He had seen life nurtured by obscure, everyday happenings. Little wonder that the characters' efforts to define their own Jewishness are often more suspenseful than the carefully managed suspense over their escape. To a great extent, *The Wall,* with most events recorded at the level of the archivist's curiosity, is understated as *Hiroshima* was. Levinson, of course, has the authority to understate that Hersey lacked, the authority of memory. So effective is this delegation of authority that I. L. Peretz, as quoted by Levinson, can speak for Hersey when his words suggest that the Jews' resolution of the ghetto experience could be a pattern for a community of man, a human response to inhuman oppression. These are close to Hersey's own pleas for international understanding, even his membership in the United World Federalists for the life of that group. Some reviews of the novel cited mistaken politics as well as mistakes in detail,[11] a failure to give one or another ghetto resistance group due credit. In Israel in 1951, Hersey would meet Warsaw ghetto survivors, some of whom had read *The Wall* in English and offered him candid criticism.[12]

"A journalist is not allowed to be confused," we recall Hersey wrote years after *The Wall* was published; "he must *know*."[13] And if he is truthful and humble, he writes within what he knows. Such a journalist, however, acknowledges the complexity beyond those limits. "Fiction," Hersey continued, "is not afraid of complexity as journalism is." This statement points to the differences between *Hiroshima* and *The Wall:* the report is restricted to the survivors' accounts against the objective information available when the article went to press; the novel leaps into the complexities of the ghetto and all of Jewish custom that lay behind it. The complexities flow forth in Levinson's fragments, and any simplification, any semblance of sure knowledge that may be derived, has come cumulatively and been stated glancingly a thousand times in the midst of a fiction. Finally, as his archivist is momentarily distracted, Hersey has another character make his point: "*Nu,* what is the plan for tomorrow?"

Chapter Three
Making Things Up

In trying to tell the truth, the literary artist must dare to lie, to make things up.

—Hersey, introduction to *The Writer's Craft*

Although he would still take on reporting assignments, Hersey had become primarily a novelist as he finished *The Wall*. He wanted at this point to write more imaginative fiction than the novels of contemporary history he had completed, partly goaded by critics and even more driven by his own creative restlessness. His success with *A Bell for Adano, Hiroshima,* and *The Wall* had barely whetted his eagerness to see what he could do with the possibilities of fiction first revealed in his year of postgraduate study at Cambridge. The rapid-fire storytelling of *A Bell for Adano,* the arrangement of the Hiroshima survivors' interviews into a continuous account of the bombing, and the "invention of a memory" were steps in the making of a novelist beneath the burden of his historical conscience. Ironically, the four novels of this new creative period would be undervalued by critics and ignored by most readers of Hersey's popular early books.

Each novel Hersey wrote in the 1950s was a significant attempt to do something different. No two of the four novels are alike or like his earlier work, except that they all treat moral issues seriously. Each can be read only so far as a novel of contemporary history, and that aspect may have frustrated some admirers of *The Wall.* For example, while there is some trace of the McCarthy era witch-hunts in *The Marmot Drive,* the moral tale that Hersey intended to have "go all the way over to imaginative literature"[1] is no political allegory. Aside from their formal variety, these novels illuminate Hersey's treatment of the most persistent subjects in his work. *A Single Pebble* foreshadows *The Call* in considering the impact of Western technology—and Western dreams—on China. *The War Lover* is about warrior psychology, a subject that eluded Hersey's reporting and fiction during the war itself. *The Child Buyer* is his indictment of American public education in the fifties before the full fury of its failings hit him at Yale in the sixties.

The Early Stories

Hersey's short fiction has come in two spurts. His first eight stories were published between 1946 and 1950 and written before the greater part of his work on *The Wall*. The second flow has followed *The Call* in 1985 with no sign of abating. The early stories, although appearing at the height of Hersey's postwar celebrity, show a young writer of fiction attempting both simple and subtle exercises in his craft. In the best of these pieces he seems less concerned with announcing urgent truths than with mastering a particular writing problem he has set himself. Sometimes, as in the narration by the title character of "Peggety's Parcel of Shortcomings," his delight is unmistakable.

Two stories derive from Hersey's postwar assignment to China and have much in common with character sketches contained in his reports to *Life* and the *New Yorker*. "The Pen" is a simple moral tale, marred by a vague ending. While a troop transport is docked in Panama, a very young seaman second class goes through a passenger's belongings and is about to walk out of the stateroom with a "Monel metal" fountain pen when he sits down to write his name. The act stirs his conscience, and he crosses out his signature, tosses the pen into a locker, kneels, presumably prays, and leaves. Soon the cabin's occupant, a "huge . . . , tired-looking" civilian doctor, returns, misses his pen, and reports its loss, offering the scrap of paper as evidence. Hersey contrasts first the penitent would-be thief with his punitive would-be victim, then the victim's rage and bewilderment with the navy's apparent indulgence of the sailor, and finally the sailor's continuing contrition with the doctor's notifying no one when he finds the pen in the locker. The doctor, alone in his hotel room after the transport reaches Shanghai, removes a navy towel from his suitcase, showers, and discovers, after he has finished unpacking, that his pen is gone. Hersey makes some point about the worth of the "Monel metal" object, but he ends with the pointless mystery of its disappearance. Could the young sailor, so ennobled by Hersey's earlier contrast, have returned to the room to make away with the pen? Did some other sailor manage the theft with fewer qualms?

"Why Were You Sent Out Here?" offers a contrast developed more through character than through plot, and a subtler ending than in "The Pen"—without loose ends. Two American colonels in Peking,[2] one thirty-five and the other sixty, engage separate rickshas to take them from their hotel to headquarters. The younger man is full of talk, mostly about himself, while the older man is reticent. Predictably, the older colonel recognizes an earlier self in the talker and recalls his own insolent vitality in similar circumstances.

As the officers reach their destination, Hersey adroitly manipulates perspective. The reader sees first the younger colonel bargain glibly and amicably with his driver and then the older one, supposedly wiser for his recent perception, hand his driver some unspecified sum that sets the man screaming at his heels. Suddenly he turns and hits the driver with a swagger stick, and walks away, in uncomprehending fury after handing him a thousand-yuan bill. The reader sees clearly that the younger colonel is bound for better things while his older colleague cannot face up to the reasons he was sent out on his present assignment. In this story, Hersey was obviously free to make up details and pursue the elusive truths beyond what he could observe for "Two Weeks' Water Away" and other dispatches about American servicemen in postwar China.

"The Death of Buchan Walsh," which is Hersey's first fiction about writing, concerns a difference between fiction and journalism. As a reporter, he could back up whatever he wrote about someone with what he knew about that person; as a storyteller, he was drawn to make up more than he could have learned from getting the facts. The narrator in this story is a writer living in suburban Connecticut at about the time Hersey was an overseas correspondent for *Time* and *Life*—someone with the leisure Hersey did not then have for writing fiction. In the midst of work on a story about his friend, Buchan Walsh, the writer gets a call from his subject begging him to come down to the city and help him resolve a love affair. In New York, the writer discovers, unsurprisingly, that his story anticipates some of his friend's circumstances, and rashly brings the couple to his home, the setting for the next episode he has planned. Of course, what actually happens is unlike the details in his notes, and after Buchan and the woman separate, the narrator drops the story. Years later, Buchan is killed on night reconnaissance in Germany. Lost and under fire, his last message had been that he intended to stay where he was. The narrator has failed to imagine, or perceive, the inertia that was the meaning of Buchan Walsh's life and death.

Hersey was one of several writers and other artists who pooled talents and resources to publish *'47—the Magazine of the Year,* hoping it might be as successful as *Reader's Digest* and *Time* had been when they started up after World War I. His only writing to appear in the ephemeral publication was "A Fable South of Cancer," which reads a bit like a condensation of the utopian novel it could have been had Hersey not been committed to *The Wall.* It begins with an aircraft carrier running aground on a desert island. The crew survives intact and votes to remain lost, unanimity prevailing until they argue about whether to destroy radio equipment or store it—to found a new world or hedge. Government is entirely democratic, with rank and privilege vanish-

ing as individuals show their abilities, and this commonwealth prospers un-
changed until a majority finds life unbearable without women, whereupon
radio transmitters come out of storage. In no time, the carrier's crew members have become another small nation squabbling to the brink of civil war.
At the end of the tale, Chief Burlingame, the elder statesman whose body is
tattooed all over with great sayings, feels a great itch between his shoulder
blades and asks his wife to read the accompanying text: "Men are only as
good as their deeds." Whatever he might do, his wife says, would only put off
trouble for a while. A while added to a while, he replies, could be the beginning of a good long time. The point is more persuasive in this story than it is
in "Alternatives to Apathy," which Hersey published in *UN World*. In that article, "ten things that one man alone can do" amount to a course of study and
action that could lead to effective advocacy of a stronger United Nations. The
fable, for all its meandering bluntness, is craftier in every sense of the word
than the urgent article, whose tenth commandment is to "reinforce convic-
tions with courage. . . . It takes courage to act, and only by action on the part
of individuals, only by going on from the basic steps outlined here to really
coordinated political action on local, national, and international planes, can
the present trend toward war be reversed."[3]

"A Short Wait" and "Peggety's Parcel of Shortcomings" are both about a
woman's view of experience, making the major character of each story its center of consciousness more than Mrs. Nakamura and Miss Sasaki were in
Hersey's account of their reactions to the Hiroshima explosion. Both stories
go further into their characters' consciousness than Levinson's recordings of
Rachel Apt's views of her transformation in the Warsaw ghetto did. They anticipate Hester's point of view in *The Marmot Drive* and, however remotely,
White Lotus's narration in the novel bearing her name.

Luba, the main character of "A Short Wait," is a survivor of the Lodz
ghetto, arriving alone in New York after several months of delays in arranging her passage to the United States. Her aunt and uncle, who had sponsored
her immigration, are not at the pier to greet her or on hand when she reaches
their apartment. Hersey then attempts the subtlest, most delicate situation in
all of his fiction to that point. The courageous young woman begins to feel
sorry for herself and resentful as she imagines her relatives ignoring the letter
she wrote them during the worst days in the ghetto. For an instant, the reader
may share her outrage that any safe Jew—that *anyone*—could have been un-
moved by her appeal. ("I could have known. We could have known.") Luba,
with steely restraint, asks the maid whether her aunt and uncle had ever mentioned the letter and learns that, instead, they had received no word of her
until after the war. Hersey's accomplishment lies in portraying Luba's aware-

ness, in an instant of reflection, that this is true and her moving joyfully to greet her aunt and uncle upon their belated arrival. The story remains one of Hersey's most moving tributes to Holocaust survivors.

"Peggety's Parcel of Shortcomings" stands out from Hersey's early writings for its humor, even for the humorous working out of its lighthearted sexual symbolism. It is the story of one night's whirlwind romance, told some years afterward by Peggety, the pastry cook, who weighs in at "two oh eight" and appears content with a life of snacking on delicacies she has set aside from her work. Her glorious blind date with a gallant boatswain's mate half her size was complicated by an errand for her employer that found her toting a fragrant piece of salmon all over Manhattan on her wondrous night. The package started out as the symbol of all her unhappiness and became her lucky charm; though the boatswain loved and left her, the night granted her lifelong self-esteem. "How was the fish the next night?" a listener asks. Miss Peggety replies that she "rested a morsel against [her] palate . . . , squeezed out a sob . . . and said to [her]self, 'I'm not so bad as I thought, not half so bad.'"[4] The story was a rare, even sly bit of larking for Hersey that almost conceals his successful experiment.

The Marmot Drive

Hersey was not a complete recluse in the early 1950s as he settled down in Connecticut to write novels. Although he avoided literary society in New York, he served on local school boards and worked in several capacities for both of Adlai Stevenson's presidential campaigns. Perhaps his most significant action in those campaigns was to collaborate in the writing of Stevenson's 1956 speech calling for a nuclear test ban. The 1963 treaty against open-air and underwater tests followed from much more than this speech, but Hersey's contribution recalls his plea for action in "A Fable South of Cancer" and "Alternatives to Apathy."

Measured by his deeds, Hersey has been one of the most politically active American writers since the 1930s. His campaign work at national and local levels for liberal Democratic candidates, steady as it has been, is less significant than his political actions in behalf of educational reform and civil rights. He is not, however, a political novelist to be compared with his early admirations, Malraux and Silone, because his political writing usually urges such actions as his own instead of treating deeds as the embodiments of political ideas. *The Conspiracy,* written just before Watergate and set in Nero's Rome, is the closest Hersey comes to a novel like Malraux's *Man's Fate,* in which a political idea is dramatized as the hero's choice to die for the dignity of others.

Neither Hersey nor any other postwar American writer has had the political opportunities of the writers of the thirties, but Hersey, unlike Norman Mailer, has not tried to cut the figure of a Malraux with the political opportunities at hand. One cannot imagine Hersey, at his most earnest, writing such a personal narrative as *Armies of the Night*. In fact, one cannot imagine Hersey in the early fifties trying, as Mailer did, to live what he had missed in the thirties and write such a fable of Trotskyism as *Barbary Shore*.

In the grim months after Stevenson's first presidential campaign, when Senator McCarthy's allegations of Communist subversion were becoming shriller, Hersey plunged into the writing of his third novel, *The Marmot Drive*. It was his first book since *Men on Bataan* that was not based on what he had seen as a reporter, and it had no more factual underpinnings than his research into Connecticut town histories.

The story is told from the point of view of Hester, a Manhattan office worker on a weekend in the remote Connecticut village of Tunxis, where she finds herself under scrutiny as her escort's "serious girl." Her self-consciousness heightens and distorts her observations of a woodchuck hunt (the "marmot drive" of the title), which brings out the fears and meanness of the villagers. Her love affair becomes unexpectedly complicated by her attraction to her father-in-law, Matthew Avered, the village selectman. This situation develops in a rural New England of piercing lights and gloomy shadows reminiscent enough of settings in Hawthorne's tales[5] to suggest that Hersey, too, is allegorizing, and, given Hersey's earlier subjects, the temptation is to read *The Marmot Drive* as allegory, even topical allegory. But Hersey is not so artful with abstractions as Hawthorne, and *The Marmot Drive* is seldom as clear, on any level, as Hersey's prior fiction.

Hester first sees Tunxis as a shabby place, "a dull little station of gray clapboard, hooded by magnificent elms, and across the way . . . half a dozen store backs, cheaply built structures crowded together with a squalid, tenemental look far out of key with the clean landscape of tilled valleys and traprock cliffs through which the train had come . . . , just another montage of soft-drink signs, tar-paper shingles, gas-station pennants, and grinning billboards" (10). The village has men and women to match its landscape. They are like the seventeenth-century New England settlers in William Carlos Williams's *In the American Grain,* huddled together in "the bigness of their littleness," at odds with the New World. Exceptional persons among them will, like the Selectman, be scorned for "having too many buttons," and when the woodchuck menace grows in Tunxis, some people will react as viciously and fearfully as other Americans did in the security alarms of the early fifties.

They are, in fact, remarkable for their cruelty. Nothing describes them so well as Hester's remark that they "are so hard on each other" (220).

The woodchuck hunt shows the villagers at their worst and the Selectman at his most isolated. It is he who must recognize that an emergency exists when woodchucks infest gardens, overrun Thighbone Hollow, and appear ready to walk right into people's houses. It is he who must remind Tunxians that it is a civic duty to clean out the rodents and who finally becomes a public scold in the town meeting, parrying objections tinged with personal insult. The respectable people of Tunxis can hardly restrain themselves when they are faced down by their chosen leader. "As if they resented his intelligence and wanted to destroy him for it" (9), Hester muses. The fate of Stevenson's wit in the 1952 campaign was fresh as Hersey wrote this.

Everyone is assembled at dawn in four divisions (Hester and young Eben Avered in separate units) to surround the woodchucks and drive them out of their hollow. Hester, finding herself alone in the confusion, has more opportunity than she can handle to know herself and Eben against the backdrop of his native surroundings. But her perspective is limited on this foggy morning and grows altogether distorted when the sun breaks through and the woods become an "Equatorial jungle" to the city girl who works in an air-conditioned skyscraper. The story of the hunt lurches back and forth in the maze of Hester's impressions and sudden appearances by the Selectman, Eben, and an odd assortment of villagers: Anak Welch, the giant; Roswell Coit, the lecherous town bully; and Mrs. Tuller, the virago who leads Hester's division. The people who had been reluctant to join the hunt are now clamoring to kill woodchunks and bored by the Selectman's strategies for finding them.

Frustration boils over the second day, when the weather warms up and the animals remain in hiding. The Selectman persists in leading, now more openly determined to finish the job well. "You mustn't think that I'm some kind of Captain Ahab," he tells Hester. "The drive's just a practical measure" (104). Most of the first woodchucks to be sighted bare their teeth and escape. The villagers now resent the Selectman's failure in the field even more bitterly than his reasoned argument in the town meeting the night before and begin looking for an occasion to make him their scapegoat. The exceptional man is perforce a complicated man in Hersey's scheme, and if his neighbors cannot outface him in a meeting or on the field, they will fall back on the methods of their Puritan ancestors. The novel begins and ends at the village whipping post, a barely credible relic to Hester when she first notices it at the foggy beginning of the drive and the altogether fantastic upshot of her weekend in Tunxis.

From the moment she first saw him, Hester compared the Selectman with
his son, finding differences as she struggled to see likenesses. Listening to
them argue, she opposed the father's values to the son's, the village to the
city,

the father living in the world of stern education, personal reticence, love of nature; of
respect for property, idiosyncrasy, privacy, and poetry; of literal horsepower and the
slow walk; of rigid family life; of frugality and thrift, of the Classics and the Bible, of
charades and early-to-bed,—the son living in a prosy, urgent, intrusive world, a
world of "realities": of revolution everywhere, of wars and military preparings and
posturings, of fear for the future; of cities and science, of jets, reactors, and ultra-high
frequencies; of cool rationality and nervous breakdowns; of the shifty images of TV;
of ads, giveaways, strained budgets, gadgets bought on the installment plan; of
speeding tickets and drunken picnics and sexual frolicsomeness in the small hours.
(105)

Hester herself dismisses these lists as too simple, even if they are mostly true,
and balances them briefly by acknowledging "qualifications and shadings
and loopholes." The difference that eventually almost consumes her has little
to do with these men living in different worlds. Eben has been a chaste suitor
despite her occasional teasing; within hours of arriving in Tunxis as Eben's
"serious girl," she finds herself strongly attracted to his father and excited by
rumors of girl chasing in his past. Rarely on the two days of the marmot drive
does she see Eben or hear from him, while the Selectman admits that this circumstance has followed from his own plan to see more of her. Gradually, the
habit of comparing Eben at all abstractly with his father gives way to fantasies
of seducing the Selectman. Hester tells herself that she wants to get him alone
so that she can understand Eben better, but soon imagines his embraces "here
in the woods. He was experienced, compassionate, troubled by day-
dreams. . . . It would be wonderful . . . , not here in the snarled vines, of
course, but in the soft-floored forest" (127). The reader must surmise from
the Selectman's speeches and actions whether he has any inkling of Hester's
fantasies and must then consider whether he uses her to punish himself in the
unfolding of village justice.

Hester and the Selectman come together by an abandoned church, whose
long-dead Parson Churnstick had driven parishioners away in his "off-and-on
crazy moods" and submitted finally to being shut up in a cage whenever
these moods came over him. The last time Matthew Avered had come by this
church, with its tilting steeple, the Selectman had been so startled by the sight
of a woodchuck tottering down the aisle toward the pulpit that "it was one of

the things that made me want to go ahead with this drive as soon as folks would cooperate. Church is no place for a woodchuck. I could just picture one of them up in the pulpit giving forth on morality and damnation" (217). Not only has the Selectman sensed a parallel between Parson Churnstick's situation and his own, if not his affinity with the caged eccentric, but he has obviously never overcome guilt feelings for earlier dalliances. Hester apparently has not sensed his uneasiness as she confesses to being "all mixed up," unable to learn what love is, possibly because the times are against her. Sometimes, she admits, the Selectman seems to mean more to her than his son does. What can she believe? she asks him, What is love? The man she has fancied as an idealist as well as a lover replies that he is still trying to find out, having failed to see that God is love and that he can offer Eben and Hester no better advice than to "struggle along on whatever leftover ethics [they] can scrape up" (222–23).

Shortly afterward, at another site in the woods, in another thicket of fore-shadowing parallel, Hester submits briefly to the advances of Roswell Coit before drawing back in shame at having chosen so "to punish the Selectman." Hours later she is alone again with the Selectman, trying to see "something else she can scarcely define" in his compassion as he works to remove a speck from her eye. Ironically, Mrs. Tuller, who had once told Hester that Avered's great weakness was that he loved all of his townspeople, spies them in this compassionate action and is stirred into a fury of suspicion. The villagers soon have their scapegoat where they want him. Matthew Avered is arraigned with dispatch and sentenced to a "light public whippin'." (Woodchucks actually appear at the edges of this gathering and slip away as the decree is announced.) Everyone except Hester (presumably, even Eben) turns to the punishment with astonishing decorum, and the accused is whipped, then left to return to the hollow, where the townspeople laugh at him as he stumbles about, flailing at woodchucks.

Hersey has conjured an anachronistic incident that compels an allegorical reading, as Shirley Jackson did in "The Lottery." A reader—even the first readers of *The Marmot Drive,* eight years after the Nuremberg trials—no more believes in a "light public whippin'" in a twentieth-century New England village than he would believe in the possibility of a woman's being stoned as a ritual sacrifice in such a setting. In fact, since Hester has turned away from the scene, the punishment is not described, nor is the sound of the scourging, nor are bloody scars afterward, only Matthew Avered's vague, "faraway look" when he leaves the platform.

But the story has been told from Hester's point of view, and its resolution must come with whatever state of mind she takes away from her weekend in

Tunxis. The apparent injustice of the Selectman's punishment is therefore clouded by her inability to shout out his innocence, just as his attitude toward her is less certain because of Hester's infatuation with him. Unfortunately, the reader may be as baffled as Hester when she says, "Besides (what a confused and mean comfort!), why was the Selectman so passive? Was he really somehow guilty of something?" (261). What was the burden of Matthew Avered's exceptional quality, which is, after all, as much the subject of this novel as Hester's weekend or the woodchuck hunt? What was Hester's awareness of the weekend as she decided to "fly away from what she had learned about herself" and from "the Selectman's image"?

Almost all reviews of *The Marmot Drive* were unfavorable. The book was commonly perceived to be dull and obscure, a journalist's failure at writing a novel. Had Hersey been more of a celebrity, or more a celebrity-novelist, he might have been the public failure that Mailer was with the reception of *Barbary Shore:* author of *The Naked and the Dead*—the combat novel about the meaning of war, not just what war was like—now out with a muddled book, apparently about dead ends in Trotskyism. Hersey was spared the publicity that followed Mailer's widely reported efforts with his third novel, *The Deer Park,* and his remarkably and bravely self-revealing anthology, *Advertisements for Myself.* In comparative privacy, Hersey could put the bad reviews for *The Marmot Drive* beside the exhilaration of having written it. He had attempted something vastly more difficult than the straightforward narration in *A Bell for Adano* and than the complications he had bypassed when he invented Noach Levinson to tell a story that he, John Hersey, had no authority to tell himself. The story of *The Marmot Drive* was his own invention, and what he learned in writing it is evident in the extraordinary variety of the fiction that followed it. In the best of that subsequent work, the strength of Hersey's craft is as clear as the seriousness of his ideas.

A Single Pebble

In 1953 Hersey was elected to the American Academy of Arts and Letters, along with E. E. Cummings and Roger Sessions. At thirty-nine, he was the youngest writer ever to have been chosen. The honor confirmed his reputation as the author of *Hiroshima* and *The Wall* at the same time that the society belatedly recognized the poet who had written so vastly different a war novel as *The Enormous Room.* In the mid-1950s Hersey was an active member of other writer's organizations as well as the Academy. As head of the Authors League Commission on Censorship, he reported in 1955 that censorship had spread farther in the previous two years than it had in the preceding two decades. Such were Hersey's professional actions aside from his writing in years when many of his colleagues held teaching positions and undertook lecture tours.

In June 1956 Hersey published *A Single Pebble,* a very short novel as lucid as *The Marmot Drive* had been obscure. He wrote it in an agony of mind over whether he would ever see China again now that the Communist revolution seemed to have sealed it off indefinitely from Americans. The story has some basis in a downriver trip on the Yangtze he took in 1946 with *Life* photographer Dimitri Kessels, even to the presence of an American engineer as a fellow passenger, but it owes more to nostalgia and exile and other feelings in the time when China was America's "lost love." The phrase describes a strange mixture of Americans who lamented China's alienation from the West: missionaries' children like Hersey, fearing they might never return, and those like Henry Luce and Rep. Walter Judd, who championed Chiang's dreams of reconquering the mainland; the head-hunting congressmen like Joseph McCarthy and William Jenner and the men, like Owen Lattimore and General George Marshall, they accused of handing China over to communism.

Hersey's instincts as foreigner—white devil in Tientsin, mishkid in New York and New Haven—surge in this book, coursing through his depiction of the failures of both Western technology and Western meliorism. *A Single Pebble* is about what the narrator, an American hydraulic engineer, learns as he travels up the Yangtze on a junk from Ichang to Wanhsien, a stretch of the river where the upward-bound traveler first encounters the awesome Yangtze gorges. The engineer recalls a time when he "and the century were in their twenties" and he was full of a plan to dam the river and thereby solve what he perceived to be China's greatest problems. He not only worshiped technology but believed in the miraculous power of a single massive technological effort. Presumably, the narrator tells his story at the present time and has some perspective on World War II and the bombing of Hiroshima—although Hersey never alludes to specific events in the narrator's life after his twenties, and one can only infer from the narrator's tone that he has lived to question the impact of either the bombings or his cherished dam.

The engineer was even naive enough in his twenties to feel that he needed only to inform the Chinese of his plans and the dam would rise as quickly as method and machinery would permit. He carried this thought all the way across the Pacific and a thousand miles upstream from Shanghai. (Shanghai, on the Whangpoo just south of the mouth of the Yangtze, was the port of embarkation for journeys like the engineer's.) Thereafter, the engineer traveled by junk and, to be entirely accurate, by the labor of trackers, those coolies taken aboard at Ichang and put ashore wherever the current or the narrows might require the vessel to be pulled upstream.

The engineer boarded his junk before dawn, only to wait all day and all night until it pushed off at the next daybreak. For twenty-four hours (his measurement and no one else's) he was "held in a prison of others' patience" while the cook went ashore to buy cabbages. No one seemed to mind, not even the owner, who stood to lose money from any delays. The young engineer, for all his irritation, was not at all surprised, because what he understood confirmed all the stereotypes of Chinese backwardness that he had brought along with him from America. As the only idle person aboard, he eventually looked down from the imagined dam to the human beings who shared the deck with him. He began to learn about them before he had the opportunity to survey the gorges for his site; sometimes the knowledge he gained distracted him from his visions.

Four persons emerged from the Chinese surrounding him: the cook, the owner, the owner's wife, and the head tracker. The cook appeared to behave impudently, even irrationally. He sang and shouted antiphonally to the trackers' rhythm, raucously quarreling and joking with the head tracker. He was cynical about everyone's motives, including his own, and apparently indifferent to any danger on the river. The owner was like a Western ship's captain except during tracking operations. Then the trackers' movements were so geared to the head tracker's commands that the owner, on his conning deck, could only wave and shout to please himself. A fatalistic entrepreneur, the owner knew that the river absolutely ruled his existence, and he therefore seemed unconcerned with speed or profits. No one aboard the junk was less interested in the American's talk about a dam.

Su Ling, the owner's young wife, was bound to her marital duty, although she was desperately in love with the head tracker. The engineer also found himself strongly attracted to her, perhaps sexually. She was his listener who could respond with folklore and poetry. Samuel Girgus writes that she "provides the impetus for [the engineer's] own self-exploration."[6] When she was not busy with her husband's comfort, Su Ling had more time than anyone else to converse with the American. Although she was not at all flustered by the Western passenger, he hardly knew what to make of her. Aside from her wide-open eyes, her appearance was not striking, but in her conversation, which could begin grudgingly, she became "a well of understanding and learning." The engineer had to listen closely, check his impatience and, eventually, an impulse to seem prepossessing in her eyes. He related his visions to her by the hour, more aware in his narration years later of the horror beneath her gentle replies.

Old Pebble, the head tracker, personified the centuries of boatmen on the Yangtze that would vanish with the engineer's dam. He struck the engineer at first as a human beast of burden. To the American, it was inconceivable that Old Pebble could have any attachment to his own "Sisyphus life." He catechized Old Pebble. What does he do? He pulls a towline. What is his future? He has very little. What are his goals? He will stay on boats because there will always be someone to hire him, and, when he dies, all of his brothers in the boatman's guild will pay for his funeral. "I thought that he might be dramatizing himself as a poor, pure-hearted wanderer, one of Heaven's minstrels, to me, a foreigner who asked questions," the engineer relates. "I could not imagine that a young, vigorous, and cheerful man could live without distant goals: wealth, family, and a name widely known" (14).

When the narrator mentions Sisyphus, one wonders first whether the myth of the endless labor occurred to him when he saw Old Pebble in the twenties and then how much he had understood the tracker over the years of reflection before he told his story. The tracker's work is both a struggle with the river and a long-evolving harmony between generations of trackers and natural forces. It is better explained by the Way of Tao than by the myth of Sisyphus. When the junk is towed past hazardous points by Old Pebble's skill and daring, the tracker and Su Ling speak of the river's being propitiated by sacrifice, yielding to those who love it. Oblivious of impropriety, even sacrilege, the engineer put his vision of the dam to Su Ling in familiar terms: his technology could so change life on this river that no junk could ever possibly be wrecked, and there would never be any need for trackers. Nothing could so change the river, she replied calmly. She would be marked for life for having heard his impious suggestion, and she added that it would kill Old Pebble were he to hear it. The engineer listened and forgot: "as the days passed, and I began to see what a dam could mean to the human beings on the boat on which I was traveling, particularly to the trackers, the dam became more important to me than it had been when I had approached it as something theoretically and technically desirable, as an abstraction in a company memorandum and in the minds of some faraway engineers" (91–92).

At Witches' Mountain Gorge, "the longest, most beautiful, and most mysterious of all the chasms of the river," the passage narrowed to 150 yards across. Trip after trip, it was, obviously, the great test of Old Pebble's existence and his supreme happiness. When a very young tracker slipped from the tow path into rough water and got his foot wedged between rocks, Old Pebble leaped instantly to his side and freed him. Days later, the engineer's admiration for this act led him to approach the head tracker as he was repairing the parrel of his harness and praise his handiwork. Ignoring Old Pebble's wary response, the engineer tried to say that a bronze and wood pulley would be a hundred times more efficient for holding a towline, but he could not come up with the Mandarin word for *pulley* and instead went on more extravagantly about the triumphs of Western machines. The next day the engineer found the site for his dam:

Between those two sheer cliffs that tightened the gorge a half-mile upstream, there leaped up in the imagination a beautiful concrete straight-gravity dam which raised the upstream water five hundred feet; much of its curving span was capped by an overflow spillway controlled by dam gates and tube valve outlets, and a huge hydraulic jump apron designed to pass unprecedented volumes of water stood ready to protect both the dam and the lower countryside against the freshets of springtime. Ingenious liftlocks at either side carried junks up and down on truly hydraulic elevators. The power plant was entirely embedded in the cliffs on both sides of the river. The strength of the Great River, rushing through the diversion tunnels that had been used for the construction of the dam, and through other great tubes and shafts bored through solid rock, and finally into the whirling gills of nearly a hundred power units, created a vast hum of ten million kilowatts of light and warmth and progress flowing through high-hanging wires over six widespread provinces. . . . Beyond the tall barrier, junks sailed forward with their wares, to Chungking and beyond, as on a placid lake. (107–8)

The engineer, driven by his Western demons, described his dam to Su Ling and Old Pebble exactly as he had just seen it, dwelling on each detail to the limit of his Mandarin vocabulary. Then he conjured the sight of the transformed river as he had before to Su Ling. Old Pebble stood up as if to strike him but instead began speaking to Su Ling and the cook in a different dialect, abruptly willing the engineer out of shipboard existence. To the narrator's surprise, both Su Ling and Old Pebble spoke amiably to him the next morning, as they stood together watching a coolie lash a spar. There was some jostling, and later on the engineer found that his pocket watch was missing and surmised that someone had used this reconciliation to steal it. Su Ling and Old Pebble dismissed the possibility of a theft, but the engineer easily imagined that Old Pebble had seized it as an affront to his machine worship. Su Ling, terrified the day before at the engineer's description of his dam, was furious over his accusations. She, not Old Pebble, called him a "foreign devil," as though to ostracize him from the human company on the river before the approach to Wind-Box Gorge, the last and most dangerous tracking passage before Wanhsien.

The haul at Wind-Box Gorge began with "errands of superstition"— burning ceremonial papers and running bells and pennants up the halyard.

Even the owner made a gesture of bringing his closed fists together and bowing to Old Pebble, his "Noise Suppressor." Old Pebble led tracking songs as the junk proceeded inch by inch up the visibly rising level of the river, his tone becoming so urgent that even the engineer sensed the forebodings that Su Ling had expressed since she first heard of the dam. The climax of the engineer's reminiscence comes suddenly. When the junk approached the end of the gorge, he looked up the side of each cliff. The trackers were above the river on a hand-cut path that had "a ceiling, an inner wall, and a floor of solid rock, with only peril for an outer wall." The engineer wondered how he could "span . . . a millennium in a day," his first admission of an unbreachable distance between himself and the Chinese. He tried to imagine their patience: "Suppose I had been called upon to cut a stone path like this for fifty years of my life, to be relieved then by my son? What if I had been called upon to haul a junk through this path all my life?" (139–40). Then he noticed that the path had been cut to just the height of a tracker bent forward in his harness. This image of equilibrium between man and river, centered on the head tracker, vanished when the engineer saw Old Pebble stare at the opposite cliff. There, rising perpendicularly to the river, were square holes along the sheer cliff face, one above the other in a zigzag pattern to a height of seven hundred feet. They had been cut with hammer and chisel by soldiers of the Eastern Kingdom, in the Sung dynasty (during the late Middle Ages of Europe), who then placed timbers in the holes to build a ladder for trackers to tow their trapped ships out of the gorge. Before the engineer could reflect on this feat,

Old Pebble broke into the most amazing song I had ever heard from him; a whirling, spiraling sound of pure joy. It seemed to me to be wordless. He was pulling now with all his strength; he held an arm reaching forward, as if that would hurry him. Still he looked across at the marks on the reddish cliff. . . . His face bore a look of great happiness or great pain—much like the faces of people caught in photographs of terrible disasters, their mouths drawn by agony into seeming smiles. His song was thrilling. He strained wildly at his harness. (145)

At that moment, Old Pebble slipped and fell flat forward. As the next tracker pushed his ankles aside, Old Pebble tried to loosen his harness so that he could get out of the way, but it would not give and he fell off the edge of the path. The trackers strained at their ropes, with their leader suspended below the ledge twenty feet above the river, until the owner screamed for anyone with a knife to cut Old Pebble loose so that the junk could move on. Su Ling moaned inconsolably, but only the engineer appeared to question the decision: "I felt a desperate love of life, of my own life, and I watched the slow gnawing of the bamboo hawser up there. If that was a minute, it was a very long one. It made me come close to sensing the meaning of the most awesome concepts: paralysis, burial, infinity" (154). In his consternation after Old Pebble was cut loose into the currents, he hardly noticed the owner leap into a sampan and hopelessly set off to recover the tracker. Wet and filthy, the owner burst in upon him the next day in Wanhsien at a banquet the American gave the crew, brushed aside his thanks, and, like an angry ricksha driver, demanded and got more money for the trip. The story ends with the engineer awake that night, feeling "pangs of wishing and despairing" and hearing "an itinerant story-teller with a crude shadow-scope, a kind of stereopticon that I had seen in towns downriver, and I heard him wail out his advertisements of famous things to be heard and seen at the modest charge of one round copper coin" (181).

A Single Pebble is a philosophical tale drawn equally from Hersey's complex, passionate bond with China and his brooding over the use of technology. He was not merely inspired, as he had been in *A Bell for Adano,* by an urgent story to be told, nor was he burdened, as he had been in *The Wall,* with an assumed obligation to atone for everyone's ignorance of the Holocaust. As later writings confirm, especially "The Homecoming" and *The Call* (almost thirty years after *A Single Pebble*), the possible failure of the Protestant mission in China—the failure of his father's work—underlies Hersey's story of an engineer who failed as an evangelist for Western progress. Because Hersey let his imagination play freely over these ideas and his Chinese memories, *A Single Pebble* is his most nearly perfect fiction, if not a greater book than the larger novels that have provoked more attention—*The Wall, The Call,* and *White Lotus.* It is clear, straightforward, and profound, told by a narrator free of any certainty about the meaning of events that have changed him forever.

The War Lover

Hersey wrote his first attempt at a war novel, "Sail, Baker, Dog," while he was still aboard the *Hornet* on his first combat assignment. Little wonder that the carrier pilot, who was the model for his hero, was offended by Hersey's central character or that Hersey would be chastened by the implication that he was ignorant of his subject. What was remarkable was Hersey's choosing, in those times when everything else he wrote was so adjunctive to the war effort, to write about men who lusted for war. There had been no suggestion of war lovers in *Men on Bataan,* even in the portrait of MacArthur, and none had appeared in *Into the Valley* or Hersey's other reports from Guadalcanal. The Japanese were often "Japs," even "Jap bastards," in those writings, but the American military that Hersey portrayed took no special joy in killing them. Hersey's typical combat serviceman fought only to end the war and return to a normal civilian existence.

For the Christmas edition of *Life* in 1943, Hersey wrote the text "Experience by Battle" that accompanied a gallery of combat paintings by artists on assignment. His comments on aviators make amends to the offended *Hornet* pilot: "American fliers are not cruel or insensitive, far from it. Most of them are naturally gentle, kind, and generous. If they do not talk much about the damage they do, it is because their job is impersonal. It has to be. . . . The war will end sooner for aviators, and their scars will heal quicker, if they can concentrate coolly on hitting the enemy carefully."[7] Hersey's interviews of the Hiroshima survivors, even when Dr. Sasaki states that those responsible for the bombing should be tried as war criminals, do not contradict the notion of efficient and impersonal American aviators. Obviously, Hersey could not begin to understand the horrors related to him at Klooga and Warsaw as warrior psychology. General Patton's ghost never haunts *Hiroshima* or *The Wall,* but Major Joppolo's does, as Hersey's books on the ultimate horrors of World War II become devoted to the survivors and builders of a new existence. Almost fifteen years after Hersey's last combat journalism, he offers such a man, a peace lover, as the narrator of *The War Lover.*

Lieutenant Charles Boman begins his tour in England as a typically "gentle, kind, and generous" flier and becomes, well before his last mission, a determined survivor who specifically rejects the notion that "the war will end sooner" if he "can concentrate coolly on hitting the enemy carefully and well." He vows instead to go beyond merely saving his own skin to doing "all [he] could to help [his] companions get through the tour alive, but . . . nothing . . . that contributed to the death of anyone" (339). *The War Lover* is basically the story of the struggle between Boman's love of life and the lust for killing that becomes his pilot's death wish. Boman declares a "separate peace," not quite as Frederic Henry did in *A Farewell to Arms.* The woman Boman loves has shown him that he would be incapable of loving her did he not love life as well. Whereas for Frederic Henry life was finally a "biological trap," the nothingness following Catherine Barkley's death, for Boman it is at least the chance to return to Daphne and persuade her that they can "make a life." This is the humanism that, as most readers of *The War Lover* observe, contends with the perverse mechanism that Boman's pilot, Buzz Marrow, represents.[8] Marrow has named his B-17 *The Body* and flies it as though he were touching it, each mission a sexual arousal begin-

ning at briefing with "little yips like those of a happy fornicator." It takes
Daphne to show Boman that Marrow's behavior is sickly confusion that can
lead only to self-destruction.

The War Lover consists of alternating sections of narrative: "The Raid," a
tense account of the twenty-fourth mission, and "The Tour," Boman's recollections of preceding missions and his affair with Daphne. Both are told in
the same state of anguished reflection brought on by Daphne's revelation of
the pilot's terrible secret and, as devastatingly, how she secured it. The conflict between Boman and Marrow, and what each man represents, is evident
from the beginning, and the resolution of that conflict—Marrow's fate on
the last mission—is just as clear soon afterward. Hersey invests Boman's
story of himself with whatever drama and suspense there are in this novel,
making the starker figure of Marrow, as well as the inquiry into why some
men love war, incidental to the narrator's development.

At 0235 of the day of the Raid, Boman is awake two hours before he is
scheduled to be called. "War equaled s—[In 1959 Hersey still used dashes in
obscenities that many contemporary writers were spelling out] and peace
equaled s——" (17), Boman muses in despair and nothingness.[9] Not only is
"the old Marrow" out of mind, but "the old Daphne" may have slipped away
too, as images of death pervade Boman's thoughts. From his boyhood, he re-
members a corpse washed up on a beach; then the sight of his friend Kid
Lynch, still in the crippled bomber that had just landed at the base: "The
world, this f—ed-up ball of s—we lived on, had blown the top off his skull
and thrown all of him away." Still, on this bleak morning Boman notices
black skid marks on the runway twenty feet below him as *The Body* lifts off;
in his agony, he turns instinctively to these signs of safe return from mission.

Marrow, on the other hand, seems never to think about survival. He is apparently all vitality and bravado; impenetrably egotistical, he commands the
worshipful attention of the whole crew because they believe his undoubted
flying skill will bring them through the tour alive. Even Boman finds himself
beguiled by Marrow's flying long after he has learned that the man is perverse. "Just seeing that thing makes me feel horny," Marrow says of his plane.
Claiming a little later to have made love to three nurses while in flight, he
adds: "Flying's as good as getting it, and when you do it, too, bang, bang"
(69). He almost never mentions the war. "To Marrow war was a simple matter," Boman states. "It concerned his potency, his destructiveness. That there
might be human beings with him or against him scarcely entered his
head".(72) Boman gains some idea of how fully he differs from Marrow
when he goes cycling with the unit meteorologist beneath a brilliant blue sky
and finds how much in common he has with the earthbound weatherman

with whom he talked about the flight of Icarus. The meteorologist was "content to imagine the Blanchard balloon with its curious feather-like oars drifting across the English Channel. With Buzz it had to be speed, daring, records, accidents, death, self. For Marrow the vault of heaven was only a mirror" (77–78).

Boman is with Marrow when he meets Daphne at the base, unaware she has come to a dance as a "dead man's drag," her flier having been lost on the day's mission. He is fascinated by her perfunctory mourning: "She was in love—not with poor Pitt any more, but with everyone, herself, life. . . . I had the illusion, however—and whether or not I was justified, I clung to it, a lamp-post in my reeling world—that the only person to whom she communicated real feeling was me" (92). Boman retains this illusion as their love grows, but he also gains something of the radiance he perceived in her that first night. England becomes more than an air base and its surrounding towns: "I had come to have vivid, powerful feelings about all that damp green plate of landscape, seen in many lights. It had meant, so often, departure toward danger and then arrival back to safety; parting from Daphne, perhaps for the last time and the prospect of reunion, relieved and weary, glad to be alive for her sake" (95). Daphne becomes the heart of a mystique of living that embraces rooms where the two have stayed; English towns, rivers, and countryside; the Tate Gallery and the Cambridge madrigal singers. Hersey, who had not been in England during the war, draws fondly from memories of his postgraduate year at Cambridge in 1937. But neither Daphne nor England is a sentimental attachment; to Boman, whose duty time leaves him little to imagine but death or survival, free time with Daphne offers the delight and challenge of living within complex and subtle feelings that lead to endless discovery. In one conversation about their pasts, he suddenly understands something new:

I was not listening to her too carefully, for I was thinking of what I could tell her next to impress her with my sensitivity, my kindness, my warmth, the ideality of my parents, my high regard for everything. Daphne was trying to impress me in the same way, I guess, and probably she was not really listening to me, either. But strangely enough, each of us, so concerned with our own excellent qualities, came through that conversation to appreciate each other more than before, even though we took in little of what was said.

This feeling of self-love, the first step toward the love of someone else, was a source of inner strength for me, and I wanted to let Daphne know that ever since I had been in this room with her the last time, I had felt stronger, more sufficient to my tasks. (136)

In this exhilaration, Boman brings Marrow with him one day and listens to him tell Daphne the story of his life, a coarse, monotonous account of women he has taken to bed and the planes he has flown. "But what about the war?" Daphne asks him. "Never had it so good," Marrow replies. "I like to fly, I like the work we're doing. . . . Boman here and I belong to the most destructive group of men in the history of the world" (136). This is too blunt a speech, obviously, but the whole scene shows how Hersey has made his title character Boman's foil and even their conflict a step in Boman's development.

Marrow has acted strangely since takeoff on the twenty-fourth mission. He is silent when ordinarily he would be cursing the crew over the intercom, and then he turns vindictive in a whining monotone until everyone ignores him. His face and his eyes take on strangely fixed expressions. Boman, without hesitating, orders a silent Marrow to kill fuel to an engine when it is hit. In the next emergency, a crewman appeals directly to Boman, and the copilot realizes that he is now in command; Marrow is relegated, as the mechanical man, to purely manipulative actions. He manages a last "miraculous reflex" before he loses even routine instincts and Boman motions him to the copilot's seat.

With Boman in command of the flight, the narration returns to the tour and Daphne's disclosure of what went on with Marrow in her room. The pilot had arrived uninvited with his Distinguished Flying Cross (DFC) in one hand and a fifth of whiskey in the other, vaguely belittling Boman as not "real gutsy . . . too educated or something," before turning to his abiding themes of speed and fighting, the cars he had owned, and his mad money—two fifty-dollar bills, which he suddenly tossed on Daphne's bed. Then, to Boman's devastation as he is told the story, Daphne went to bed with Marrow, her love of life drawing out his perverse secrets in order to destroy him. Hersey sacrifices some credibility and a few of the illusions he has nourished about Daphne and Boman so that he can propose an autoerotic basis for Marrow's behavior. Daphne insists to a distraught Boman that Marrow did not "really" make love to her, because he was like an earlier RAF war lover she had known who had "wanted to use [her] to make love to himself." Her unresponsiveness had driven Marrow into a torrent of recrimination. He admitted that Boman was actually capable and courageous but that while his own DFC was undeserved, under no circumstances should Daphne think that he, Marrow, was cowardly. "I didn't care where the f—we dropped those bombs, as long as it was on a city," he shouted at her. "You can't win a war being squeamish. Chicken s—doesn't win wars. You have to kill *somebody*" (381).

At that instant, Daphne interrupts Marrow to tell him that she knows all about him. She knows all about the feeling he has, "that stirring down there

. . . that wells up out of the dark, slimy place of toads and snakes and hairy men" (382). But, Boman wonders, had she gone that far with Marrow just to learn this? Her answer is not at all comforting. She had also gone to bed with Marrow because life goes on and Boman's tour was ending, and she had come to feel that Boman had not wanted her much more than Marrow had— differently, of course, but not much more. She asks Boman to consider just what he had meant by "selfless love," or whether his commitment to their happiness was not as shaky as the compromise he had worked out for himself on bombing missions: to go along, but do nothing to help kill anyone. Boman leaves the apartment heartsick, however Daphne may have enlightened him about his pilot.

Returning to his account of the raid, Boman recalls ordering Marrow to be trussed up in the radio shack and issuing orders before a crash landing in the Channel. He analyzes him a last time: "*The Body,* his body as he imagined, had been opened up to let death in. He was maimed. His power and manliness were not untouchable at all; they were being taken away from him. Because of the inner drive for death he did not know he had, he passively welcomed his emasculation and disarmament" (396). Boman last mentions Daphne as the English coast comes into view:

I loved England. I wanted England. Dimly in the distance I could see the tall bluffs of the east coast, the stretch from Dover to Margate, where the glare path of the sun ended in shadow. . . . I wanted a miracle to buoy me to England. . . . I wanted Daphne. I wanted, just once more, to be with my Daph, to lie on my back in a meadow by a sluggish stream, with my head in her lap, talking about us. Couldn't I see her once more to tell her I'd meant to handle things differently? I wanted another chance at life. Couldn't a man try again, and get it right this time? (399)

The Body hits the water, submerges and splits in two, and then briefly rights itself, the forward half at the surface. As he gets out and pulls away from the wreckage, Boman sees Marrow bobbing against the fuselage. He swims up to him, and Marrow pushes him away, clutches a propeller blade, and goes down with his ship.

Although the action closes in "churning spindrift," the survivors are men left with every possibility that may begin once the rescue craft have picked them up. Boman chooses to end his narration while he is still adrift in the Channel. He may get back to Daphne, and they may make a life together. Or they may not. Hersey might have written a much simpler novel focused on Marrow, whose last act might have taken all hands down in *The Body,* save Boman, cast out like Ishmael. But as we have seen, Marrow, no Ahab, was driven by no greater demon than orgasm, physiological or psychic—so flimsy an obsession that Daphne's revelations may have rendered him the zombie he was on his last flight. Hersey chose instead to follow Boman's anxieties to a point where his mere survival left him able only to imagine the premises of a new existence. *The War Lover* is the reflective war novel that Hersey could not write as a war correspondent or in the postwar years he gave to writing *The Wall.*

The Child Buyer

The Child Buyer denounces the abuse of intelligence in American public education and often flares as a satire of other American institutions and purposes. Its subtitle suggests a distant similarity to the form and intention of Jonathan Swift's "A Modest Proposal": "A Novel in the Form of Hearings before the Standing Committee on Education, Welfare, & Public Morality of a Certain State Senate, Investigating the conspiracy of Mr. Wissey Jones, with others, to Purchase a Male Child." *The Child Buyer* takes the form of a hearing transcript to develop the irony of a society's persuading itself to turn a bright child into a commodity—a machine of superhuman, if not artificial, intelligence. This intellectual and spiritual cannibalism, elaborated with some conventional novelistic suspense, is understandably less shocking than the real thing proposed by Swift's narrator, nor do the several speakers at the hearings combine in a tone at all so memorable as the single narrator's righteous rationality. Hersey packs a novel's plot and several satirical targets into his transcripts, which barely hold up under the burden, however vividly one may recall committee hearings on television. Nevertheless, Hersey's satire has become more relevant since its publication, with advances in robotics and speculation on "downloading" the mind into computers.[10] His suggestion is at least as plausible as when he wrote it: that Americans are so incapable of living with genius and so responsive to any appeal in the name of "national security" that any of them could reach a point where he would justify selling a child like Barry Rudd to a corporation like United Lymphomilloid for the purpose of making him into a computer with all his senses "tied off" so that nothing can distract him from reaching an IQ of 1,000.

Among Hersey's efforts in the 1950s to write a novel about education was a draft of several thousand words describing an extraordinary teacher of gifted children.[11] This character, who became Mildred Gozar in *The Child Buyer,* was based on "women who loved kids and wanted to learn from them" in the Cleveland school programs Hersey had studied as a member of the Connecticut Committee for Gifted Students. His many other activities in public education also fed into his writing. School board service made him familiar with budgets, hiring and firing, and building specifications, as well as curricula and methods. For more than ten years he learned about testing, guidance, and "enrichment."

His most pressing interest in education was always the situation of bright children in a democratic school system. In his own schooling, it should be noted, a bright child was usually well-off, whether in Tientsin or at Hotchkiss, where one English instructor steered Hersey from Galsworthy to Faulkner.[12] Neither he nor anyone he knew in school was a neglected prodigy. His first writing on anyone like this was "The Brilliant Jughead," a *New Yorker* article tracing the progress of an enlisted man through a U.S. Army school for illiterates. Hersey reported how this man, among thirteen thousand service personnel, had mastered the equivalent of a sixth-grade education in three months of intensive work. As he toured public schools later on, Hersey would remember that the proverbially impersonal U.S. Army had taken great pains to identify the merits of each illiterate soldier. Classes never dragged as civilian instructors balanced their presentations between informal conversation and exacting drill. Hersey was especially impressed by the graduates' appreciation of the program. "They can take away my gun, also my uniform," his "jughead" said, "but they won't ever take away how to read and write."[13] Nine years later in *Life,* Hersey attacked the "distortion of the philosophical assumption of 'teaching the whole child.' "[14] He found that the cult of wholeness had spawned such a phrase as "language arts" to replace "reading and writing." Teachers too often encouraged mediocrity by failing to push bright students into more difficult study and instead offered them "enrichment" through correcting spelling papers and straightening out filing systems.

That writing which most anticipated *The Child Buyer* was "Intelligence, Choice, and Consent," a report commissioned by the Woodrow Wilson Foundation. In it Hersey describes the plight of "Janet Train," a twelve-year-old girl from a lower-income family whose high verbal ability was ignored by careless testing, indifferent school officials, and, most of all, the prevailing concept of egalitarianism. It was a difficult conclusion for a liberal to reach, but Hersey was convinced that the noblest democratic intentions were no guarantee of good education.

According to Hersey, the very fact that Americans recoiled from any sign of preferential education led to their embracing mediocrity. Teaching had become pitched to the mythical average student. Norms replaced ideals. IQ tests, which originated in thoroughgoing experiments by Binet and Terman, encouraged inane imitations that could be used by anyone interested in screening out talent. Professor Bagley of Columbia Teachers College even used an IQ range of 85 to 115 for his definition of the common man. A democratic system had produced schools that could not help sustain a democracy in a world where most other nations paid special attention to their brightest students:

The work of the Manhattan Project in developing the atomic bomb seems to have convinced many people that all that is needed to unlock supreme mysteries, such as cancer or talent, is an act of Congress, or the banding together of many vast agencies, and expenditures of huge sums of money. But the job of freeing talent does not lend itself to this kind of attack. Ability is elusive; genius wilts in a bureaucratic setting. Intelligence of a high order is mysterious, manifold, fast-moving, luminous, tantalizing, and incredibly beautiful.[15]

Hersey tries to counter democratic bias against exceptional intelligence by arguing that bright students can be found anywhere in society and by suggesting in his notes on Janet Train and her once-bright mother that a sympathetic environment can make a great difference. Intelligence, he states, is, like vitality, fluid and variable and dependent on the emotional life of the person in whom it is found. He calls for a genuine equality of opportunity to replace a muddle of good intentions. But most American school officials, he felt, echoed the school superintendent in Janet Train's town: "I'm afraid of anything too special for these clever children. I'm afraid of it for our city. We don't like anything that smacks of privilege. But don't worry, we reach those children . . . with enrichment.[16]

Thus Janet was enriched by filing papers and went home to read her sister's movie magazines. Democratic education, Hersey argues, should welcome the unexpected intelligence that cannot be measured easily. The anger that would conceive of the conspiracy in *The Child Buyer* bristles in the last passage of the report:

The failure here is a failure of national vision—for we have tended to see human beings as statistics, children as weapons, talents as material capable of being mined, assayed, and fabricated for profit and defense. . . . The only sure defense of democracy will be its inner growth, and the first essential of this growth is something far less grandiose but far more difficult of realization than the National Defense Education Act, or a crash program under any other title—namely, a true recognition that each child in each classroom in our schools is a unique human being, who one day must make choices and give consents that will help to perfect us all.[17]

Barry Rudd, the nine-year-old prodigy in *The Child Buyer,* is not simply a slum child with an IQ of between 130 and 144, as in Janet Train's case, but, certifiably, one mind in a million. His greatest interest is taxonomy, "the family, genus, species, and sub-species of every bird—of every living thing you could imagine—in Latin." While he has the principal's, Dr. Gozar's, respect and his classroom teacher's affection, Barry languishes in a school system filled with caricatures of the egalitarian officials cited in Hersey's Wilson Foundation pamphlet. The guidance expert boasts of a twenty-minute test offering the equivalent of three years of psychoanalysis. The evasive school superintendent cannot make a coherent statement because he cannot use simple connectives to link the blocks of professional jargon floating in his mind. Into such a community, Wissey Jones enters as a talent scout for United Lymphomilloid. He has only to whisper "National defense!" for the state senate committee to hear his opening testimony deferentially. By the time he reveals his company's full plan in a closed session, most people with a hold on Barry Rudd have agreed to sell him. The force of Hersey's satire depends on a reader's believing that even Dr. Gozar and Barry's mother are vulnerable at some point to Wissey Jones's sales pitch. The bright children sold to U Lympho are sealed in dark, barren cells, six feet square, for a period of several weeks, seeing and hearing nothing except piped-in whisperings of the goodness of U Lympho—"the motherly, protective, nourishing qualities of the corporate image, and later . . . Her creativity, fecundity, and later still . . . Her Great Mystery—the Miracle of the Fifty-year project"—all as they are being dosed with "L. T., *lethe terrae,*" forgetfulness of all earthly things. These preliminaries are followed by "education and desensitization in isolation," whereby the subject is put into a small room with no windows, never again to "look out at the complexity of nature, which would only confuse him." The subject's "whole life becomes an attempt to please Her by spurts of creative mental activity, which are seen as worshipful acts." Then the subject is transferred to three weeks' data processing by calculating machines that in turn have been fed by previously conditioned specimens:

The subject is now perfectly prepared to do Her work. There are, however, two dangers. One is that through some inadvertence, unforeseen by the minds of the technicians who have not been conditioned as the specimen has, scraps of information that are not wholly related to the subject's particular area of worship-solving may creep into his mind. The second is that he may develop emotions: it has been found that, despite the prophylaxis and enthohexylcentron, extremely dangerous emotions may arise, apparently stemming from tiny doubts about Her, the source of which Project researchers have not yet been able to pin down. The specimen therefore undergoes major surgery, which consists of "tying off" all five senses. Since the subject need not take in any more data, he has no further need of sight and hearing. Smell and taste have long since been useless to him, since he regards the intake of food as a mechanical process that he carries on only for Her sake. Only so much sense of touch is left the specimen as to allow him to carry on his bodily functions and write on a simplomat recorder, a stenographic machine, the use of which has long since become a ceremonial rite for the subject. Most subjects are also sterilized, though a certain few will be left their reproductive equipment in order to breed further specimens for the Project. (207–8)

In the final stage, "productive work," the subject comes up with "solutions of incredibly difficult problems relating to the Mystery." Not even the child buyer himself knows what the Mystery is, although he believes that it has something to do with "man's greatest need—to leave the earth." How, a senator asks, could that relate to national defense? Jones reminds him that U Lympho is under government contract and ventures to observe that "in the present state of affairs the best defense might be departure."

The plot leads not to this disclosure but to a succession of points at which each person with a hold on Barry Rudd—and at last, Barry himself—agrees to the sale. "Everyone . . . asks—and usually gets—a price," Wissey Jones deposes at the first hearing, and everyone is eventually paid off, except Superintendent Owings, who is so caught up in his own rhetoric that he does not hear the proposition.

The guidance expert quickly accepts an assistant superintendent's position under an aging Superior in a wealthy district. He had chosen guidance as his field because he believes that it offers rewards teaching cannot match. Tests are his passion. He is particularly fond of the Olmstead-Diffendorff game, an "improvement" on the "verbally-loaded" Stanford-Binet tests because it consists "entirely of problems developed by cartoons in comic-book style, and [draws] for content on the child's world of television, sports, toys, and gadgets, [and it] is 'culture-free' and without social bias" (46). Barry's mother, once a bright child herself, keeps a slovenly household and sees her son's genius as her compensation for her lost hopes. The boy's father, who began to work for a living when he was Barry's age, is eager to sell. Mrs. Rudd's breaking point is reached brutally when the child buyer stages a hoodlum attack on the Rudds' tenement. In her anger, Mrs. Rudd shouts obscenities in front of her children and instantly loses any lingering self-respect. Jones pays her off with cultural tokens: "the best works of man . . . the Five-Foot-Three-Inch Classics Shelf . . . the *Drawn and Quartered Quarterly,* the digest of all the biggest Little Magazines . . . and a new television . . . so we can view The

Endless Mind. . . . All the cultural opportunities I've ever dreamed of" (245).

Miss Frederika Gozar, Barry's principal, seems thoroughly invulnerable to the child buyer. A paragon of hard-boiled virtues, she holds four master's degrees and a Ph.D., sleeps only four hours a night so that she can spend four hours in a biology lab before going to her desk in the morning, knows almost everything Barry Rudd knows, and, of course runs her school with absolute efficiency. She rephrases some of Hersey's statements on intelligence. "I believe in the infinite potentiality of young people," she testifies, "and I think I can do something about it." After all, she was the person who had discovered Barry and saved him from enrichment by letting him work in her lab. She gives in finally through intellectual pride, the defect of her virtues: "Barry's finished as far as . . . what he has called home is concerned . . . [;] the chance of something remarkable being salvaged at United Lymphomilloid seems to me worth taking. And if he fails, if he does forget, and if they do turn him into a machine, he'll be the best." (250–51) The brightest adult in Barry's world is made to show how humanism can betray itself in its struggle with mechanism.

The final party to the agreement is Barry Rudd himself. His IQ is 189 (Stanford-Binet, tested at age five), approximately that of Bentham, Leibnitz, Macaulay, or Grotius, and higher than that of Voltaire, Descartes, Darwin, Newton, or Lope de Vega. It is masked by a pale, impassive face set upon a fat, slow-moving body. The shrewd Wissey Jones describes Barry: "When words that stand for strong feelings pass the short, tight lips, only a flicker of expression, like distant heat lightning, can be seen around the eyes, which are startlingly clear, direct, and alert." (30) No description could prepare the reader for Barry's testimony. In his first utterance under oath, he admits that he is a skeptic. An array of his curiosity follows:

Miss Henley reminds me of the word, "bipinnatifid." I'm not sure why, unless it's that Miss Henley uses the first-person singular pronoun so much, and there are four i's in bipinnatifid. . . . When I was in the second grade, I saw a brown thrasher for the first time, *Toxostoma rufum,* and heard it sing its song, like a mockingbird's, only funnier, truly humorous, and I didn't know what it was, so I described it to my teacher . . . and she showed me the color plate, Common Birds of America, in the big Webster, and I remember that "bipinnatifid" was at the top of the opposing page, and I looked up its meaning, and that got me interested in leaves and their comparative forms." (74–75)

His taxonomies are touched by poetry:

I only know I'll never be as happy again as I was the other afternoon in the woods. The white oaks made a backdrop, because, you know, they hold their leaves the longest, like small leather gloves, still solid green; while the elms and hickories had gone brown early in the dry August we had this year, and in the wind on [hurricane] Ella's train the week before they'd been almost stripped, and their skeletons made a blackish mesh, so the displays of the other trees seemed even more prodigal: deep coppers of the sumac and dogwood, pure yellow of the birches, and, here and there, ironwood and sassafras, and, best of all, the incredible orange glow of hard maples— like the inside of a Halloween pumpkin when the candle's lit. (77)

Faintly, Hersey traces Barry's growing awareness of the child buyer's errand and how he becomes convinced that any further life for him in the town would be meaningless. Although he learns about the procedures of the U Lympho project, he decides that life there might "at least be interesting." This is the high point of *The Child Buyer,* Hersey's culminating irony that gathers all his feeling about the impoverishment of bright children in American public schools. Their classrooms are Forgetting Chambers in which "enrichment" kills curiosity, and the system, in its ill-conceived egalitarianism, resembles the inhuman project.

When this "novel in the form of a committee hearing" works well, as in Barry's concluding testimony, Hersey's irony subdues and even exploits his didactic impulses. The basic fiction of the hearing does not work as well as the frame story for the conspiracy to sell a male child; characterization and plot develop in response to questions put by inadequate or incredible questioners. Two of Hersey's state senators are cartoon figures—an imbecile and witch-hunter—while the committee counsel and the chairman are undeveloped and useless after early hints of roles they might play. The title character is hard to accept as a kind of satanic road agent, Mephistopheles on a collapsing motorcycle, snaring even the redoubtable Dr. Gozar but forever denied his employer's innermost secret. Finally, what if Barry Rudd had been simply a bright child instead of the peer of Leibnitz, still full of the beautiful and elusive intelligence that had engaged Hersey's sympathy? Would not the betrayal of such a mind have been a stronger indictment of the democratic tragedy of American education and even as effective an object of satire as the mechanization of genius?

In the *New Republic*'s symposium on the novel,[18] B. F. Skinner, who invented a teaching machine and experimented with a "baby box," was understandably struck by the force of Hersey's distortions. The situation in *The Child Buyer,* Professor Skinner wrote with apparently unintended irony, was implausible, the work of someone who "has been trying to do something about education." Carl Hansen, then superintendent of schools in the District of Columbia, complained of "satire, as it always is, at the expense of balance." Hersey, according to Hansen, should have known that education, at the working level, "demands more good sense than most people think. . . . Is knowledge now becoming man's master?" Such attacks on *The Child Buyer* hardly needed to be offset by praise from others in the symposium.

Chapter Four

White Lotus: "an extended dream about the past"

This work is not intended as prophecy; perhaps it should be thought of as an extended dream about the past. . . . It is, in short, a history that might have been, a tale of an old shoe on a new foot.

—author's note, *White Lotus*

In 1962 while Hersey wrote *White Lotus,* he chose the contents of *Here to Stay,* the first collection of his magazine articles. The title indicates a thematic basis for his selection that he expressed several times in a brief preface: "I believe that man is here to stay in spite of the appalling tools he invents to destroy himself" (vii). He chose a theme that had run through most of his writing, including the novel in the making, and that hit his readers with new force in light of the Cuban Missile Crisis, which occurred while *Here to Stay* was in press.

At almost every point in all of these writings, Hersey describes how one person behaved when his will to live was tested. In "Over the Mad River" Mrs. Kelley chooses to be rescued from her tenement apartment during a flood when the means of rescue seem far more dangerous than staying put. In "Journey toward a Sense of Being Treated Well," the Fekete family escapes Budapest immediately after the suppression of the 1956 revolt, almost house by house ahead of the police. In his note before "Survival," the well-known *New Yorker* account of John F. Kennedy's exploit as commander of PT 109, Hersey states that Kennedy took strength from "the courage-giving force of a sense of community" as well as from the fresh discovery of inner resources.

"I have been obsessed, as any serious writer in violent times could not help being," Hersey writes in the preface to *Here to Stay,* "by one overriding question, the existential question: What is it that, by a narrow margin, keeps us going, in the face of our crimes, our follies, our passions, our sorrows, our panics, our hideous drives to kill?" (viii). Perhaps nothing else in *Here to Stay,* even the reprinted *Hiroshima,* offers the existential answer as fully as "Tattoo Number 107,907," the story of "Alfred Stirmer," Auschwitz survivor. (Hersey had thought of writing more about this man before he undertook

The Wall instead.)[1] At the beginning of the war, Stirmer is a proscribed Jew living in Berlin under the severe restrictions imposed on Jews. He, his wife, and his three-year-old son must live in a one-room apartment and may not attend public entertainments; he must walk several miles to work because Jews are not permitted to use public transportation. Eventually, the racial laws outweigh Stirmer's usefulness in the German work force, and he and his family are sent off to camp, where they are separated.

Stirmer finds himself marching off to work details, snatching chances for lighter work, and making other fine calculations about how to save his energy. He seems to have determined how he will survive, partly from the conviction that the Germans will lose the war in an imaginable limit of years and months that he will have to endure at Auschwitz. What torments him is that he has no idea of what will happen to him after mere survival. Will he fall in love again? Will he ever have another three-year-old son? Where will he go? Will he survive only for the sake of revenge? Can a human being will to live toward utter uncertainty? Can he will to live with no other promise than merely being alive the next moment? The story of Stirmer's survival leads to the trials of the heroine-narrator of *White Lotus,* carried in slavery to the Yellow Empire, where she begins in nothingness to define a new existence.

Hiroshima, is grimly appropriate as it appears in this collection, published barely three months after the superpowers' brush with annihilation. "Man is here to stay—IF," Hersey notes, and goes on to cite briefly the force of three explosions: Hiroshima, a test in the summer of 1962 of a device twenty-nine hundred times as powerful as the first atomic bomb, and a hypothetical nuclear weapon twenty times more powerful still.

White Lotus was published in 1965, when the recent victories of the civil rights movement seemed to be inspiring a general awareness of the long history that had led up to them. Hersey's massive novel about "white" subjugation by "yellows" was read, understandably, as a fable drawn from the experiences of African slaves and their descendants in the United States and built upon the novelist's favored theme of survival. It appeared to ask its white American readers to imagine themselves as such slaves cut off from their ancestral culture, then segregated as an inferior race. In 1965 it was easy to ignore the novel's other origins in Hersey's Tientsin childhood, when he belonged to a privileged white minority in the European settlements. Hersey said many years later that *White Lotus* was this situation "turned inside out,"[2] a dream extended from memories of himself as the missionary's child whose curiosity had led him to tip over a water cart and suddenly feel himself responsible for the anguish of the coolie shouting at him. Reading *White Lotus* topically since 1965 has also led to a serious underestimation of Hersey's craft in his most imaginative work.

This novel stands and falls on Hersey's invention of the narrator's language, which is his translation of her assimilated "yellow" speech. Like the narrator of Ralph Ellison's *Invisible Man,* this young woman tells her story retrospectively: each incident she recalls bears upon her telling as well as her tale. Speeches in her account of village life in Arizona before her captivity show no trace of American colloquialism. Throughout the slave-ship sequence, the reader is made aware of the Whites' struggles to begin understanding the yellow tongue and never of any regret they might have over losing their native language. When they are stripped and shaved by the slave-ship crew, anything that might be called their culture falls off them with their clothes and hair. Throughout the narrative, there is no reference to any American writer or, more pointedly, to any fragment of American popular culture except images from silent films and, in early chapters, strains of "The Way You Look Tonight" and other tunes in the slaves' illicit hangouts. In the indeterminate time of the novel, the slaves accept the superiority of the Yellow language and its culture from their earliest contacts with slave traders. They have vague memories of their Arizona villages but no memory of America; they are always "whites," never "Americans." When White Lotus traces her first yellow character in the dust, the chevron flourish denoting *man,* she has the power of literacy as she never has with the alphabet that she never mentions.

As a child, Hersey spoke some Mandarin, most of which came back to him as an adult whenever he returned to China.[3] When he wrote *White Lotus,* his command, or recall, of the language was like the engineer's in *A Single Pebble:* a halting but poignant stimulus to his imagination. Hersey's Mandarin was enough to inspire the creation of his narrator, who, like Noach Levinson in *The Wall,* might give the story an authority that he felt missing in his own voice. Yet while White Lotus's Yellow language creates an authoritative fiction of her education as a slave within a strange, timeless society, its very strangeness can be distracting. A conspicuous example early in the novel is the use of the uncommon word *coffle* for "slave caravan," entirely credible as the word White Lotus has learned to convey that new situation but jarringly unfamiliar to most readers at that important point in the story. Perhaps to avoid an Americanism, White Lotus refers to sharecroppers as *metayers,* but the word, however precise or justified, must be looked up or left to hang in the mind and clutter the context in which one hopes it will be defined. White Lotus's acquired language lacks the quickness, force, and humor found in the native tongue of Ralph Ellison's narrator, despite the characters' remotely similar circumstances. "I told him that if he laid one night-soil-filthy finger on my woman again I'd inscribe him again with a pork knife" is a typically strained locution in a potentially violent and comic scene. "I hide the sarcasm from my voice, a cultured flute swaddled in rags," White Lotus recalls of a confrontation with a yellow, describing just what she must do on such an occasion, but the bright metaphor could as easily apply to her whole narrative.

The novel begins with White Lotus in the "sleeping bird" stance of her people's protest movement, facing the racist Yellow governor of an outlying province. She is poised on one leg, "like a bird perched for the night," staring ahead impassively because "nothing must show on [her] face today but her white skin" (3). Although a delegation of fellow protesters huddles behind her, she stands alone so rigidly that she cannot scan the field on either side of her. She gazes at Governor K'ung, who is marching toward her at a measured pace, carrying an uplifted sword. Just as her act symbolizes nonviolent resistance and the individual struggle of every other perching bird in the empire, it is also a fitting signature to an account of her life from earliest captivity to this moment. She is now what she has made of herself from the despair and forlornness of her circumstances—an even barer and harder-won existence than others Hersey had observed or imagined. With white family, white homeland, and white god all utterly gone, her situation may seem about the same as that of the characters in *Hiroshima* and *The Wall,* but, as noted earlier, Hersey has further imagined a loss of language—consequently, of memory—even greater than that of enslaved Africans bound over to American masters.

White Lotus recalls scenes from her life as a fifteen-year-old in an Arizona village near Flagstaff. From her limited point of view, the reader must gather all facts about the United States after its defeat by the Yellow Empire at some unspecified time in the twentieth century. There is no mention of World War I or the Russian revolution, or of Japan (which apparently had no hand in the Yellow War), Europe, Mexico (a day's drive south of the village and surely another promising source of captives), or Africa. The only Americans in this tale are white, whether in America or in slave quarters in the Yellow Empire. Hersey places his story outside any familiar history, deliberately withholding any explanation of how the yellows won the war, and since his few American landscapes show no signs of destruction, there is no reason to imagine anything like a nuclear explosion having occurred. Hersey's technological distortions and anachronisms are more tantalizing. The Arizonans are silent-movie fans (who read fan magazines), Pierce Arrows move over paved highways, and the village owns a half-track bulldozer. No movies, Pierce Arrows, or bulldozers appear in the Yellow

Empire. All farming there is done with hand tools. In their drudgery, the whites have no apparent memory of their bulldozers; in their general debasement, Ford, Edison, and all the other inventors and entrepreneurs might never have existed. The yellows travel by sedan chair and ricksha; steamers ply the river, but there is no sign of railroads. The whites cross the Pacific on a slave ship that resembles a twentieth-century troop transport, but years later only junks can be seen at moorings along the Bund in Shanghai. These oddities in a story with inescapable parallels to the history of African slaves and their descendants in America are Hersey's most obvious means of making his familiar story seem strange. If the reader can enter a fluid time, he may accept more easily a slave history with familiar eras and turning points occurring within at most twenty years of White Lotus's life.

Roving agents from white slave syndicates pick off isolated villagers whenever slave markets run low in the Yellow Empire. The unnamed girl who will become White Lotus is marched along with her tribe over back routes in the desert around Palm Springs and through the San Gabriel and San Fernando valleys to an embarkation point just north of Santa Barbara. White Lotus sees the surf as "white fire coming to the strip of the sand on the bank of the sea rolling humps of dazzling white steamy fire roaring as loud as a thousand Mack trucks" (57), as an impressed African from the interior might have described his first sight of ocean—with perhaps the roar of lions for Mack trucks. Stripped, shaved, men and women packed in separate holds, the whites, from numerous sects, pray to an unavailing God.

White Lotus's life in the Yellow Empire is painstakingly traced through six stages, three as a slave and three as an emancipated white. Sketchy American landscapes are replaced by elaborate detail of Yellow cities and farms. Left with nothing of their own, the slaves begin the painful process of accepting every new thing as a token of a superior civilization. They begin seeing themselves as the Yellows see them and accept themselves as "pigs" and "sows." Here, one can appreciate how much Hersey's having been a "foreigner"—thinking himself one throughout his life, he has insisted[4]— enabled him to imagine the whites' feelings and go beyond a studious grasp of parallels between a posited white experience and an actual black history.

White Lotus's first master is an aristocratic scholar in Peking, whom she addresses and soon fully identifies as "Big Venerable Shen." (The first full name by which she is known in this narrative of her captivity is "Shen's White Lotus.") Her mistress's daintiness in fine silks and bound feet becomes a measure of her own white coarseness. She sneaks pleasures with other slaves in back-alley taverns, but her supreme stolen happiness is to feel Big Madame's gowns against her own skin. At the taverns she witnesses hollow

rituals of rebellion: slaves' fistfights within a chalk circle, symbolically circumscribed violence and fierce oaths for young men who dare only petty
theft and malingering outside it. Being bad, the slaves say, is their only revenge. Legends of sexual potency are attributed to whites, and they become
promiscuous in a desultory fashion. When mysterious fires break out in the
city, the slaves are made scapegoats and rumors spread of slave revolts at the
same time that Moslems threaten distant borders of the empire. A spate of
trials and beheadings end only when enlightened masters, like Big Venerable
Shen, decide that whites are fit only to work as field hands. White Lotus is
auctioned off to a plantation in Honan.

Hersey centers the next two episodes on an abortive rebellion, reminiscent
in some details of Nat Turner's, and on an abolitionist movement that
roughly resembles the Underground Railroad of the 1850s. The rebellion is
led by Peace, who roars: "Thou shalt not touch these locks for it is given unto
me to deliver Israel out of the hands of the Philistines . . . [and] with the jaw-
bone of an ass will I slay a thousand" (249). These scriptures are loose fragments in slave memory, because for all one may discern, this Yellow Empire is
a China never visited by Christian missionaries. In *White Lotus* as in *A Single
Pebble,* Hersey is stirred by the doubt he would eventually address in *The
Call*: what trace remained of that mission—of his father's work? To consider
that the Communist revolution might have swept it all away helped the novelist imagine the slaves' desolate submission to the yellow civilization. White
Lotus becomes one of several handmaidens of Peace, leader of the rebellion,
at the same time that Smart, one of his lieutenants, teaches her her first yellow
characters. To learn the meaning of an ideograph, however, is an ironic en-
lightenment, because where White Lotus had once bowed to force and appearances she now submits to the essence of yellow wisdom. "Am I a slave for
no other reason than I am white?" (239) she asks. As she masters characters,
the reader is given several glimpses of primitive slave culture by the mention
of folk medicine and fish fries. The scriptures on Peace's tongue become mere
watchwords of a rebellion mocked by God's own torrents flooding the landscape and driving his scattered followers to cover. Peace cries out "in an agony
of utmost surrender," but White Lotus's unspoken thoughts are more devas-
tating: "It now seemed to me that God had abandoned us not by sending a
storm, or by failing to fend off a storm sent by the yellows' deities, but rather
had decamped from within each of us, from our natures, from our worthless
white souls. Ai, yes, I felt godlessly worthless" (296).

When the rebels' plans become known to their masters, those not killed
are sold away, and White Lotus goes to the wretched acres of "Dirty" Hua, a
former overseer. As work becomes more grueling, the slaves hear rumors of

an abolitionist movement in the North and a possible yellow civil war. The Uncage-the-Finches Society has sprung up, but the emperor, seeking compromise with South-of-the-River provinces, has published his Clip-the-Wings Edict. As work at Hua's farm proceeds in narrowing cycles of weariness and the whip, White Lotus becomes infatuated with a neighboring slave named Dolphin and, in the manner of clever slaves in Faulkner's story "Was," schemes to have her lover traded to Hua. After their slave wedding ritual, Hua asserts a master's rights over her unresponding body. She becomes pregnant (not knowing whether by Dolphin or by Hua), miscarries, and is abandoned when Dolphin is killed while running away. At her most abject point, White Lotus escapes Hua in a raid to uncage finches. She and her liberators (one of whom is "ashamed of his yellow skin") follow Tou Mu, the north star, White Lotus noting "how glad I was I had always bowed to her idol" (418).

In the remaining third of the novel, Hersey traces the stages of freedom that lead to his heroine's "sleeping bird" stance in front of Governor K'ung. What happened throughout a hundred years of black history in the United States, from the Emancipation Proclamation to the civil rights movement, is paralleled by a series of occurrences while White Lotus is still a young woman. In the novel's fluid time scheme this unlikely pace of events does not matter, of course, and it may even lead the reader to consider how little change there was for American slaves throughout historical centuries.

The refugees' freedom is bitter. Yellow masses in Peking are incensed by a war fought to free "hogs," and the government must conscript its recruits. White Lotus's new lover, Rock, fails to get called up by "the number wheel," and the couple work in a white orphanage, which becomes the target of yellow hoodlums. After the war ends in an indecisive imperial victory, White Lotus and Rock leave Peking for the "humility belt" of Hunan.

Their new life in "the lower hand" of a village roughly parallels the existence of black tenant farmers in the grimmest sections of the Reconstruction South. Hersey's imagined setting derives partly from his stay with a black tenant farmer in Mississippi during a voter registration drive in 1964, which he reported in the article "A Life for a Vote."[5] As the title implies, his host, whose identity he concealed for twenty-five years,[6] lived under conditions as hazardous as any Hersey invented for White Lotus and Rock in Brass Mouth Chang, and his "life" was not merely a life at risk in 1964 but a life prevailing over a century of hard circumstances. White peasants in Brass Mouth Chang who fail to meet a landowner's quotas suffer harsh exactions, down to the confiscation of their own hoarded night soil. In this forbidding environment, Rock and White Lotus are feared as "smart pigs" and must be circumspect in their effort to "teach some of the world's better ways to the people of our race." White Lotus's school, where she subversively teaches yellow classics to white children, is raided by masked members of the Hall, who return after their mayhem to shut it down with a decree based on the prewar law forbidding any schooling whatsoever for Whites. White Lotus submits:

Then, when it was over, I told the children that the yellows were closing our school.

Ayah! My children were white children, indeed! not a sign, not a sigh. No emotion whatsoever. Guarded, cautious, hooded eyes. No comment, no protest, no questions.(526)

Believing in stereotypes of their people, the Whites begin acting them out. Rock starts drinking heavily, and he and White Lotus turn jealous and promiscuous; he almost kills a neighbor for sleeping with White Lotus, even though at the time he had raised no objection and had in fact taken the neighbor's wife. Groundnut, a beggar who had accompanied the couple from Peking, sets himself up as a priest and founds a temple, shabby except for a thronelike chair on which he sits to preach sermons in self-restraint: "Make the best of life. . . . Do not be blind to the good things around you" (532). Having long since forgotten their mission to lift up their race, White Lotus and Rock leave the village to seek their fortunes in "Up-from-the-Sea," Shanghai, a wondrous modern city.

In "The Enclave," Hersey brings his story within the historical present of his readers, as White Lotus arrives in a Yellow Empire Harlem. The provincial whites are dazzled by the gleaming buildings along the Bund and the possibility of creature comforts for themselves. "In those first days we felt free," White Lotus recalls, "despite our having to return to the stable at evening, so to speak, we roamed at large all day, filling our eyes, as if they were our purses, with the city's riches" (554). Soon enough she learns that white men must choose from three kinds of work—"tit-suck, haul-ass number one, and haul-ass number two"—as house servants, wharf coolies, or ricksha boys. A few lucky white women may work in the silk mills ("filatures," in the narrator's tongue), instead of shifting for themselves in the streets. Rare white men have done better: a few professionals, then the racketeers, and, at the very top, the impresarios of the Forgetfulness Hong, who deal in opium and lottery tickets. As Rock resists the employment open to him, White Lotus becomes a reeler at the filature and begins grasping at the enclave's offerings of happiness. Always attractive to white males, she tries to imitate the appearance of a "mix" or even a "chinkty," straightening her hair and applying yellowing cosmetics, then studying the delicacy of yellow manners as assiduously as she had the mysteries of yellow characters. She appeals to yellow liberals, who gather in salons to hear white poets, and, one of these patrons of the arts falls in love with her, whereupon she lives at the extreme point of assimilation within a system of segregation. Then, unsurprisingly, come the first stirrings of a white protest movement. A changed Groundnut has moved to Shanghai with Runner, a true evangelist whose preachings have moved the old temporizer to lead growing numbers of "sleeping birds" to demonstrate in their stance. They recruit White Lotus, who learns the exhilaration of a "freedom . . . not to be bestowed but grasped" at demonstrations still within the city before the movement spreads on to the "hard core provinces." The novel ends where it had begun, with White Lotus breaking the silence before herself and the governor. "Virtuous wisdom, gentle hand," she says softly, and the governor turns away without reply. She has won, but, as police approach her, she thinks, "What if someday we are the masters and they are the underdogs?" (683).

Her question thrusts readers from the fluid time of the narrative into the immediate chronology of racial tension in the United States and reinforces the impression that the numerous incidents recalling American black experience form one long parallel to the history of that experience. The question also echoes the last line of Ralph Ellison's *Invisible Man*: "Who knows but that, on the lower frequencies, I speak for you?"[7]

White Lotus resembles no other book so much as *Invisible Man,* yet almost every point of their similarity reveals profound differences between Ellison's art and Hersey's. Ellison's young narrator, like Hersey's, lives through events that correspond to stages of American black experience. Since his narrator is black, Ellison offers other masks on other faces rather than Hersey's "old shoes on new feet." Hersey poses a reversal of identities, while Ellison describes a denial of identity in a jungle of stereotypes. Both narrators are linguists forming their own languages from strange texts, with sharply contrasting effects on their narratives. White Lotus speaks within the limits of Hersey's "translation," whether she cries "Ayah!" or updates some classical reflection, while the Invisible Man has the full freedom of Ellison's own idiom. As one result, *White Lotus* is all but humorless, while *Invisible Man* is a profoundly comic novel.

Most reviewers disparaged *White Lotus,* and later critics have ignored it when they have written comparisons of Hersey's fiction and his journalism. The novel was "a resplendent failure" for Webster Schott, and the *Times Literary Supplement* reviewer found his energy "dissipated by the persistence of the writer's."[8] Nancy Lyman Huse has taken some of the book's alleged shortcomings as virtues in noting that "the value of this work is its didactic, labored, intricate witnessing to the cruelty, hypocrisy, and self-destruction of a pseudo-liberal racist society."[9] Samuel Girgus, in his admiring study of Hersey as a novelist of ideas, finds the book's achievement in its "so clearly depicting the relationship between the inner world of the slave and his outer situation."[10] Understandably, Hersey has been disappointed with the novel's reception. Letters about *Hiroshima* have come to him in almost every week's mail since 1946. He has had no comments from black readers about *White Lotus,* and only one question from a Chinese reader, a student at the Foreign Language Institute in Beijing who was writing a dissertation on Hersey's Chinese fiction.[11]

Chapter Five
Lessons for the Master

But the whole point is being out *in* it. Coming through it.
— Tom Medlar in *Under the Eye of the Storm*

As armies of writers became academics in the postwar years, Hersey avoided so much as a week's appointment as writer in residence. Then, in 1965 and almost on impulse, he became Master of Pierson College at Yale, accepting a five-year term as "parent on station" just in time to see the momentum from student demonstrations in Berkeley gather to sweep dissent over American universities all the way to New Haven and beyond. At the end of his term, Yale would be convulsed by its own crisis in the same spring that students were killed at Kent State. Nor was Hersey distant from events off campus in the sixties. The summer before taking up his duties at Pierson, he was for an hour the center of controversial attention at a White House Arts Festival reading from *Hiroshima* to an audience polarized by the war in Vietnam.[1] In the middle of his term at Pierson he commuted to Detroit each week to interview the young black men indicted for murder after the riots of 1967.

Although Hersey was "truly shaken up"[2] by living in Pierson during the late sixties, most of his mornings there were given over to writing, and Yale became so congenial to him that, after spending the 1970–71 academic year in Rome, he returned to teach. For thirteen years he offered two writing seminars a year, one in fiction and the other in journalism, teaching one semester and writing the next. Each class met once a week, and Hersey saw each of his thirty students for an additional weekly hour. In guiding their work and doing his own, Hersey overcame reservations that his writing might be cramped by an academic environment. By the time he retired as an adjunct professor of English in 1984, he had written three more novels and almost completed *The Call*.

Aside from his investigation in Detroit, Hersey's subjects in these years were students and writers—and even *The Algiers Motel Incident* (1968) has agonized passages about himself as a reporter. *Too Far to Walk* (1966), completed before he went to Pierson, is another version of the problem examined in *The Child Buyer*. This time the bright child is a bored college sophomore tempted, as Faust was, by visions of boundless experience. *Letter to the Alumni* (1970) was the last of Hersey's annual messages to Pierson graduates, made longer and more impassioned than the others by events at Yale that spring. *The Walnut Door* (1977) is both sympathetic and satiric in developing the romance of two dropouts who find each other in the residue of their education. The writer's situation may have preoccupied Hersey even more than the student's. *Under the Eye of the Storm* (1967), he remarked years later, is a metaphor of his own writing of *The Wall*, because the flaw in the keel of Tom Medlar's boat was like the wrong point of view Hersey used before his discovery of Levinson.[3] In *The Conspiracy* (1972), the poet Lucan struggles to learn a writer's duty in the reign of Nero. The hero of *My Petition for More Space* (1974) is a writer in a future dystopia. Early in his career as a writing teacher, Hersey edited the anthology *The Writer's Craft* (1973) and a collection of critical essays about Ralph Ellison. Both books contain his interview of Ellison, in which he asks, "Have you felt some defiance of death as a writer—in the sense that what you are making may possibly circumvent death?"[4]

Too Far to Walk

Hersey had two sons and a daughter in college when he wrote *Too Far to Walk,* but they contributed no more to this novel of undergraduate frustration than the schoolchildren whose circumstances he studied in the fifties did.[5] The children given "enrichment" in overcrowded classrooms were the early inspirations for John Fist, who found that he wasn't getting a tenth of what he should out of Sheldon College or putting a hundredth part of himself into the place. Although only a "high achiever" and not a genius, John is as bored as Barry Rudd was in *The Child Buyer.* Rote learning in some courses and impossibly long reading assignments in others have driven John to a point similar to Barry's choice between undergoing more schooling and becoming a human computer. Since John has passed puberty, he can yearn for experience beyond Barry's reach, and since the story takes place in the sixties instead of the fifties, he can be offered a full Faustian temptation by a Mephistopheles bearing potions of LSD. The satire is much angrier in *The Child Buyer,* in which the hero is a child martyr, and Barry's surmise that his future as a computer might be more interesting than more schooling is more piercing irony than anything in *Too Far to Walk,* which is playful beside Hersey's earlier books.

John is an earnest, very young Faust when his tempter asks him (as no one else has, apparently) what he wants:

So much, so much! It began, surely, with sentience . . . to *feel*, to push his personal feelings out to the limits of the galaxies, and inward to the molten pit of the center of the earth. Awareness of the entire works was what he wanted, and to encompass and understand it all! . . . The whole thing would probably be right outside language. And above all, above all: to have this with some person, with a girl. Fusion, a feeling of such closeness that one person would *become* the other. (42–43)

But he is quick to back down by attempting a joke before the Spirit of Playing It Cool tenders his wholly serious offer of all that he wants for merely his "inmost primeval soul," not at some appointed date but immediately, with an option for lifetime renewal in twenty-six weeks. In no time, the sophomore repeats Faust's oath: "Evil, be thou my good."

John Fist's subsequent adventures consist of trials on his patience before taking LSD and, after doing so, hallucinatory travels that end with the implied prospect of recovery, however boring, in places like the humanities classroom, no longer at a distance too far to walk. Hersey's underlying argument is the obvious, timeless one that there is no shortcut to the knowledge or experience John seeks. Keeping his story within the hero's sophomore year, Hersey could not come up with as satisfying a resolution as Goethe's and therefore gave reviewers grounds for claiming that he had dismissed student anxieties and undermined serious criticism of higher education. Oscar Handlin, in an unfavorable notice, stated that "far from liberating the spirit or opening the mind, education threatens to close off choices and narrow experience."[6] Reflecting the self-criticism even then under way on most college faculties, Handlin's point was, of course, not new to Hersey but an indication that he might have ended the novel too soon by implying that his hero would henceforth walk and not soar. Perhaps Hersey's reputation for being earnest, even occasionally didactic, led some disappointed readers to overlook the appropriateness of this abrupt conclusion.

Hersey's satire of academic life is the best part of this novel. The celebrated Professor Gutwillig walks backward to admire properly the student demonstrators marching toward him. Always on the side of the angels, he knows the name of each student who has been arrested. John plays "Anticipate-the-Dean" with perfect accuracy, line after line, as he is counseled to take a year off. The college town brothel, with its dormitory decor, has touches of the establishment furnished for the heroine of Nathanael West's *A Cool Million* and a chic prostitute scholarly enough to pay John Fist for his time answering her questions about student malaise: "Do I have to put it to you in multiple choice? What's the itch?" (96). And in a perceptive comic scene, Hersey has

John sleep with the lovely townie Margaret Gardiner only because she has fallen asleep listening to him talk about himself.

Hersey turns from acute observations of John's boredom and the environment that produced it to hallucinations that begin with "sweet lassitude" and breathing colors that are a "Guatemala of the secret self." The sophomore finds himself beyond any altered state that he has imagined. These fragments are followed by episodes in which John is a lecherous Caribbean beachcomber insulting "Mrs. Silk Print," an American tourist his parents' age; then a combat infantryman, presumably in Vietnam; and a communicant at a witches' Sabbath. He is paying his part of the bargain with these excursions of his "primeval id" into terrors of self-indulgence and rebellion. In these dreams, his misunderstandings with his parents, comic material earlier in the novel, are portrayed by his father's being killed by a sniper's bullet and his mother's being raped by satyrs. "Not knowing who is the enemy," the apt American catchphrase from the field in Vietnam, rings in the combat dream as the focus of John's delirium and explains why these images of his parents so strongly influence his withdrawal from the pact with his devil. In the twenty-sixth week he dismisses his Mephisto, saying that he cannot remain "on a knife-edge between hallucination and objective truth." Margaret, appearing in a burst of sunshine, has less to do with his decision than a sober preference for any reality—"for life, anyway"—over illusions of having reached the limits of experience.

Under the Eye of the Storm

Dr. Tom Medlar, hero of *Under the Eye of the Storm,* is a thirty-four-year-old liver specialist and the skipper of *Harmony,* a yawl of "broad-beamed grace . . . , an inexpensive craft with distinctly unyachty lines." He proposes to sail her with his wife and another couple one weekend, setting out on a familiar course from Edgartown on Martha's Vineyard to Block Island. His company and sometime crew is restless, and a line storm approaching gale force advances toward them overnight from Cape Hatteras. Medlar dotes on *Harmony*'s every plank and fitting, keeps a meticulous logbook, and guards a secret knowledge of the flaw in his ship's keel.

This is the situation in Hersey's most starkly philosophical novel. Elsewhere, his characters, who may be no less alone than Tom Medlar, seek or happen upon the meaning of existence within a historical context that helps define their discoveries. This is true even of those Western foreigners in China, the heroes of *A Single Pebble* and *The Call. Under the Eye of the Storm* touches "contemporary history" in the brash claims for computer technology

made by Medlar's guest, Flicker Hamden, who would put ontology on auto-
matic pilot:

"If you had even minimal communications you'd know about the squall hours ahead
of time and get into harbor and be in some bar when the thing hit."
　"But the whole point is being out *in* it. Coming through it."
　"That's real prime stupid. Human beings ought to be in better control of their environment. You have the means. Or if you had the sense you would have. This boat's
a death trap." (34–35)

As Samuel Girgus observes, Medlar is trying to escape a "repressive technological atmosphere,"[7] disgusted with himself and his specialization—with
specialization as a way of life, it should be added, to be left behind for week-
ends in which he is tested by all "the elements of existence afloat." Medlar, as
the central figure of Hersey's tale, is devoted to his own allegory of weekend
sailing.

　The first part of the novel asserts the strengths and limitations of Medlar
and *Harmony* in the ordinary tensions of his marriage and the company of
guests, who obviously expect something closer to their own notions of a
pleasant sail. That the Medlars are childless accounts for Audrey's "periodic-
ity, itself dependable, in her crying out against unchangeable things." "Her
most telling reproach," Medlar feels, "was withholding reproach, giving gra-
cious space and light and air in which his unspecific guilt could flower of itself" (16). In this way, she has been his crew in his existential pastime,
graciously assisting "Dr. Meticulous" without interrupting him. Medlar cares
for *Harmony*'s every detail, for reasons that he has kept to himself: "Having
detected his own inner bankruptcy while still young and vigorous, Tom
Medlar had now worked out a way to get through the rest of his days busily,
painlessly, and even, much of the time, in high good cheer. His way was to be
exact in little things. There was a dynamic force in the word 'exact' that had
great appeal for him. Exacticism came to this: marking off the hours this side
of death by being precise about humdrum details of existence which in themselves had no meaning whatsoever" (6). His logbook has been exact except
that it has never recorded his knowledge of the flawed timber in *Harmony*'s
keelson, a cheap piece of rotting red oak to which every frame and deck beam
(all of exotic, durable hardwoods) is attached, or any annual reminder to
check the flaw. The vulnerability of "exacticism" is suggested by Flicker
Hamden's sudden entrance abovedecks with a pirate's eyepatch, which he
has just cut from the black endpapers of the precious logbook. While
Hamden's charade mocks Medlar's earlier defense of sailing, it also suggests

that Medlar is about to sail with his flaw into rough weather that will be the first real test of his "exacticism." Hersey actually took more pains than some reviewers acknowledged to make Medlar's sailing decisions realistic, but it is the skipper's philosophical commitment that sends *Harmony* into the open sea in the teeth of the gale.

The remaining narrative is continuously exciting and as taut as Hersey's best reporting. Allegory comes from it as naturally as sheets of rain slant in from the storm:

> He threw back the hatch and climbed the ladder and rose outward into a medium of violence for which no phase of his life had prepared him.
> A brutal push from behind, foul and delinquent, like that of muggers on a night street, drove him down, and flinging out an arm as he fell he grasped the upright pipe stanchion of the boom gallows, and there he clung, astonished, sobbing for breath. . . . That's hail coming at me, he thought. The downpour had looked like rain from below, but must be hail, for it crashed against the hood of his waterproofs and stung his skin like a solid scattershot. But no; there were no pellets of ice on the deck. It was just driven rain. (106)

Such convincing detail warrants Medlar's reflections on "escape and confrontation"; as, over and over, he repeats a routine at the wheel, it is entirely credible that "Camus's rendering of Sisyphus came to him, the aptest picture of modern man" (193).

Hersey has called this novel a metaphor of writing that offers an analogy between the rot in *Harmony*'s keel and his own mistaken choice of omniscient narration in an early draft of *The Wall*.[8] When he discovered Levinson, Hersey began a new draft; Tom Medlar only acknowledges that a new keelson would mean tearing the boat apart. The analogy is, obviously, not all of the metaphor. Medlar's logbook guided him only so far, just as any writer's preparations leave him at the threshold of his work. Meticulous Medlar has attributes that Hersey, in his introduction to *The Writer's Craft*, gives to that everyday state of the writer's consciousness that he calls "the censor":[9] his capacities for planning, his critical awareness, his inhibition. The censor struggles with "the supplier," who, according to Hersey, holds "both images and affects in rich and chaotic bounty." The point of sailing, Medlar thinks on this weekend in the company of his guest who would automate sailing, is that "you got away from the world and faced the universe—your naked self in its relation to chaos" (87). It is an abstract notion until Medlar heads into the storm. At the wheel, Medlar, like the writer in Hersey's comments, "gives himself over, it seems, to some kind of struggle between the supplier and the censor. The supplier is around, almost dangerously active; the censor, who has serious formal work to do, is hard put to keep the supplier in hand."[10] In such struggle at sea, Medlar believes that the storm "is the true world," only to find when it is over that "this world" reclaims him.

The Algiers Motel Incident

Hersey's report on the murder of three young black men in the 1967 Detroit race riots begins, appropriately, with the confusion of the victims' friends, battered witnesses to the crime, staggering home from the Algiers Motel. Hersey narrates this opening section of his account from uncredited sources, interrupting it with the bereaved parents' recollections of how they had heard about the murder from these fleeing survivors. Lined up facing a wall, continuously threatened, and intermittently beaten, these witnesses knew that sometime after police had broken into the motel, Carl Cooper, Auburey Pollard, and Fred Temple were killed, probably after having been beaten even more severely than these witnesses were. What the participants remembered about the night at the Algiers Motel and how those who were not there perceived the events of that night form the matter of Hersey's report, and those perceptions generate his theme of unequal justice. In *The Algiers Motel Incident* he holds that the killings were racially motivated police executions, that the courts were extraordinarily lenient in judging the killers (at least up to the time the book was rushed to publication), and that the blacks concerned with the case fully perceived the alleged injustice.

The book is a variegated mass of details taken primarily from Hersey's tape-recorded interviews with virtually everyone who had any part in the case. At first these fragments seem organized to reflect the difficulty of establishing evidence at the same time that the racism in the incident was becoming uglier and more obvious. The third chapter, for example, covers some (by no means all) data on the case from 26 to 31 July in twenty-one sections, from four pages of court transcript to a single sentence surmising a detective's state of mind. Congressman Conyers's aide tells Hersey ("told me" is scrupulously noted beside every item the writer takes from his interviews) how the incident was reported to the Justice Department; then a victim's brother tells Hersey about seeing bruises all over the survivors' bodies shortly before a police detective repeats his earlier assertion that the three men killed were snipers. Excerpts from the medical examiner's report appear before statements from Detective Schlachter's testimony. President Johnson's insistence that his Commission on Civil Disorder "find the truth, the whole truth, and express it in [its] report" precedes a Wayne County prosecutor's statement to Hersey that the presence of two white girls at the Algiers made him think that he "recognized the odor of a case." For more than two hundred pages Hersey builds his montage of interviews, supporting documents, and surmise, holding the reader more by the force of stray detail and utterance (as when Chaney Pollard cries, "Momma, they did worse than if they caught one of them Vietnams out there" [67], upon seeing Auburey's body at the morgue) than by any unfolding exposition of these materials. The author finds this apparent disorganization inevitable when he acknowledges: "I am continuously aware that my reliance in this narrative on the statements of witnesses tends to fragment the story; it is not so much written as listened to, in bits and pieces. The sequence of these fragments follows, as far as it is possible to follow, my sense of the run of the actual events, but I must emphasize that I cannot vouch for many minor and some major points of chronology" (274–75).

Hersey is present in this book as he was not in *Hiroshima*. The unfailing attribution of testimony that establishes his continuous presence as the listening reporter makes him seem more conspicuous when, a few pages later, in reporting court testimony, he condemns "the evident failure of the patrolmen who had been present to follow the dictates of prudence, of humanity, and of standard operating procedure even during the confusion of the riot, by reporting the deaths to headquarters" (29). Hersey had been an intrusive narrator on rare occasions in *Hiroshima,* but in *The Algiers Motel Incident* he steps forth from merely discrediting a theory that the victims were executed as snipers to state that "they were executed for being thought to be pimps, for being considered punks, for making out with white girls . . . for being, after all and all, black young men and part of the black rage of the time" (236). What Hersey felt about interviewing Hiroshima survivors must be taken from the narrative he made of those interviews. Forty pages into *The Algiers Motel Incident,* he interrupts his fragmentary exposition with an essay on the special difficulty of writing about his investigation. It is a confession of white ignorance and white guilt, extenuated by an urgency that prevails over his difficulties and feelings of unworthiness, and every line reveals anxiety stirred by the riots in 1967 and exacerbated by the assassinations of Robert Kennedy and Martin Luther King, Jr., in 1968, when the book was written and sent to press. Feeling "indiscriminate fear" and "the foreignness" he had known as a child, Hersey "was deeply chagrined to discover that stereotypic thoughts lurked in corners of my own mind" (42). Stating that he would accept no money for the publication of this story, he added: "If this declaration suggests to anyone that part of my motive in writing it may have been guilt, so be it. There is plenty of guilt lying around for the taking. Perhaps the whole point of this book is that every white person in the country is in some degree guilty of the crimes committed in the Algiers" (45).

Hersey claimed that he had broken his reporter's rule of invisibility—of letting the tone of his statements speak for him—because of the urgency of his subject, but he had addressed his readers directly twenty-five years earlier from the war fronts and even in his foreword to *A Bell for Adano.* Not only "I" but "you" enter *The Algiers Motel Incident,* as when the writer interrupts himself to say: "If you have not read it [*The Autobiography of Malcolm X*], close this book now and read that other and come back to these premises, if you will, later" (42).

Hersey's trepidations over writing this book came partly from an earlier conviction that he could not write a novel from the point of view of a black man. Much earlier, he had considered writing about Nat Turner's rebellion but "didn't dare imagine that I was black."[11] Living in Mississippi in 1964 as the guest of a black farmer contributed instead to *White Lotus,* in which Hersey could imagine a racial consciousness based on his childhood memories.[12] His reading of contemporary black writers, particularly of Ralph Ellison, was apparently as inhibiting as it was enlightening. With this particular background, Hersey went to Detroit planning a broader story on the riots but was soon drawn from his interviews of city officials, "certain Negro leaders and some young black militants," to taping the words of the persons closest to the Algiers incident. He taped, instead of relying on his customary practice of taking notes, when he saw that his young black subjects trusted the microphone and the promise of unabridged taping, an open environment of sound that students of Marshall McLuhan would have recognized as a "cool medium" as opposed to the hot, linear process of note taking. And so Hersey's weeks in the late fall and early winter were split between being Master of Pierson College and commuting to Detroit for interviews on Mondays and Tuesdays that could be postponed by his subjects' being jailed again.

Hersey dedicated this book to his Pierson students, and their influence on it is apparent. Some of them in 1967 were ahead of Hersey in recognizing conditions of unequal justice and especially in distrusting authority in such conditions. As "parent on station" at Pierson half a week while researching this story, Hersey soon found himself identifying more than he wanted to with the parents of Pollard, Cooper, and Temple, even to regarding police as they would have. A friend of one of the families had led him to these people; he interviewed the patrolmen through their lawyers. Although Hersey has no comment about usage or grammar in his unedited recording transcript of the speech of his black subjects, he precedes Patrolman Paille's words with a note about Paille's being "given to appending ragtags of inchoate continuation at the ends of clauses" (83).

Hersey chose to do this book after declining an invitation to write part of the report from the Presidential Commission on Civil Disorders on the grounds that the whole report might reach conclusions he could not support.[13] One may only speculate whether he could have done more for equal justice by writing that section—and conceivably influencing the other sections—than he did by devoting himself instead to the Algiers story. It is obvious, on the other hand, that this book had not a fraction of the impact of *Hiroshima,* and would not have had even if Hersey had shaped a much better book from his interviews. In their barest outlines, these books are similar by beginning with a confusion of detail meant to lead toward understanding—of the outrageous occurrences in Detroit and the unimaginable event in *Hiroshima.* The confusion persists in *The Algiers Motel Incident* through a deliberately incoherent montage that is already much longer than the whole of *Hiroshima* before Hersey begins a full account of what happened at the motel. This structure has been more effective in fiction than it has in journalism, and its weakness here comes partly from the procedures Hersey employed in being a visible reporter. Fidelity to the record, arising from his perceived limitations on this urgent assignment, kept him from imposing essential coherence on his story, even though he interrupts the record at points to summarize and even to moralize and exhort. *Hiroshima,* by contrast, is taut as a novella, shaped both by interviewees' memories and by Hersey's creative choice of structure.

The immediate reception of *The Algiers Motel Incident* is worth noting in light of Hersey's anxieties. Robert Conot (a strange choice as reviewer, given his position with the Presidential Commission), in the *New York Times Book Review,* unsurprisingly found the book "a rush to judgment" that could have benefited from Hersey's checking materials in the commission's report.[14] Both Conot and Stephen Schlesinger, the *Atlantic* reviewer, emphasized that the book was appearing before the patrolmen had come to trial, and Schlesinger conceded, with some irony, that Hersey's "sense of idealism drove him to write this book and take the risks of boring his readers with stretches of detail and prejudicing the forthcoming trial."[15] Nat Hentoff, in the *New Republic,* suggested a comparison that was inevitable in 1968 when he wrote that Hersey was not "a writer who both puts himself into his journalism and is also complex enough (Norman Mailer, for example) to dig so deeply into his subjects and into his own ambiguity as to return sufficiently altered by the experience to reflect in himself 'the mythic themes of racial strife in the United States.' "[16] Mailer's *Armies of the Night,* also appearing in 1968 and also about a 1967 crisis, may be a more telling contrast to the Algiers report than *Hiroshima* is. This account of the march on the Pentagon to protest the Vietnam War is built on inseparable parts of the event's complexity and the writer's ambiguity. The event is distorted and the writer portrayed, often caricatured, in ways that Hersey had foresworn by choosing his method. Alluding to no transcript of his own and intermittently to the intensive media coverage of the march, Mailer is faithful to his own recollections or free with them in writing what he would call "history as a novel, the novel as history." Ten years later, Hersey would write in "The Legend on the License" that "the widespread acceptance of [Mailer's] *The Executioner's Song* as a 'true-life story' is an ominous sign of journalism's ill health these days," a "doppelganger game" Mailer had "played before."[17] *Armies of the Night* has been a more memorable book than *The Algiers Motel Incident* for many reasons, two of which matter at this point: one, it was more interesting because of how it was made up, structurally and imaginatively, and two, the writer as historian, novelist, or performer was a more vivid presence than the scrupulous interviewer.

Letter to the Alumni

Ordinary campus life vanished at many American colleges and universities in the spring semester of 1970. Demonstrating students pillaged administrative offices at Cornell, wringing concessions to their demands. Four students protesting at Kent State were killed by shots from National Guardsmen on 4 May. At Yale, in Hersey's last semester as Master of Pierson College, the proximity of the impending New Haven Black Panther trial aroused a range of student concerns that crested, as Hersey wrote in *Letter to the Alumni,* on a "historic weekend, when, to everyone's astonishment, the house didn't come tumbling down and indeed seemed to be shored up stronger than ever" (4).

Students like those Hersey met at Pierson just after publishing *Too Far to Walk* were perceiving unequal justice as freshly and as passionately as he had in Detroit. When his perceptions of the 1967 riots were threatened by biases from his earlier experience, Hersey trusted his tape recordings and the insistence of his sympathy for his black subjects. Pierson residents—particularly black residents—in 1970 had tougher choices in the semester during which "White Yale began to recognize, and perhaps even to understand, something about Black Power"(15). When the Black Panther Ministry of Information published "*To All Jive Time College Niggas*" at almost the same time that the Black Coalition of New Haven issued a statement attacking white radicals, these students were shamed for their privileged status by both a revolutionary vanguard and a group of property owners who sounded remarkably like their parents. All students had to choose between a formal course of study and its innumerable alternatives, from "Action Collective" to dropping out altogether, most male students making this choice under the threat of serving in the Vietnam War.

Since becoming master of the college, Hersey had written year-end letters to Pierson alumni in which he conveyed his impression of such university-wide changes as the beginning of coeducation in 1969 and summarized activities at the college. These letters drew so few direct replies that Hersey's sense of alumni attitudes in his 1970 report comes from "what they said at reunions" and numerous letters to the alumni magazine.[18] The distance he perceived between himself and most of his Yale contemporaries—let alone any gaps among Pierson generations—accounts for the impassioned, sometimes defensive tone of *Letter to the Alumni*. As neither a professor nor strictly speaking, a university administrator but as someone living among students, Hersey tried to write an inside view of undergraduate experience. In passing along the feelings and complaints of the young, he almost always conveys his sympathy, if not his complete agreement. He calls for "the affective side of life," citing students ("A student can say of a man who throws a public tantrum, 'at least he cares' " [30]) and going beyond them himself to ask "[a] pressing question for our universities, which had better start at least *thinking about feeling* before they are engulfed by anti-intellectualism coming at them from two sides—from their own students and from the philistines: why is this country so open to one set of emotions and their expression—rage, hatred, scorn, put-downs, vituperation, vicious criticism, character-killing; and so suspicious of, so hostile to, another—love, kindness, generosity, forgiveness, trust, praise, encouragement?" (31). Student feeling, Hersey continues, leads to "relating" and "helping," an altruism at odds with American business, which students perceive as "systematized greed." He defines the students' use of the word *relating* as "being able to give and take" and their "helping" by claiming that "a flood" of them would be out in the world to help others before, or instead of, pursuing a career.

For Hersey, "the greatest joy at Yale came with the awareness, now and then, of a successful synthesis of freeing trends" (48). Women, new to Yale, were such a synthesis in themselves when they worked to make the Mayday weekend an orderly forum. Hersey credits Yale's president, Kingman Brewster, with many of these joyous moments, but one gathers from *Letter to the Alumni* that most administrators at Yale were distrusted and most faculty remote from students when they were not hostile toward them. "It does not comfort undergraduates, who live on the ground floor, that they can hear faint strains of chamber music in the apartment upstairs" (127), Hersey wrote, with special reference to the English department and the reputation of its graduate faculty. Perhaps Mayday weekend was one of Hersey's most joyous moments at Yale because it was nonviolent, the work of students representing many "freeing trends." For that weekend, the student protests of 1970 were almost such a community as Hersey and other Pierson residents had sought for five years.

Letter to the Alumni remains a valuable record of Hersey's sympathies in his last year at Pierson. The spring of 1970 turned out to be the end of the movement he describes, rather than the threshold of either the future of repression or "the survival that is worth it," which he poses as alternatives in his closing pages. He observed years later that after the Kent State protests died down there was no feeling of sanctuary on college campuses, and, asked about the future he had imagined in 1970, he replied that we had seen government tend toward "the corporate mind" rather than repression.[19] In the fall of 1971, Hersey returned to Yale from a year in Rome to begin twelve years of teaching during which he found some students who were "bland, cynical, and selfish" and many more who were not.[20]

The Conspiracy

The short-lived Pisonian conspiracy against Nero in A.D. 65 ended with the executions of the plotters, including the writers Seneca and Lucan. Seneca, the tragic poet who had been Nero's tutor, was living out his retirement at his villa away from Rome. The proscribed poet Lucan, Seneca's nephew, lived in Rome, where he worked on his epic, *Pharsalia,* which celebrated the time of Caesar and Pompey. A few years before, Lucan had been Nero's friend. Hersey, given a year's appointment at the American Academy in Rome after his service at Pierson, drew from accounts of these events in Tacitus's *Annals* and Suetonius's *Lives of the Twelve Caesars* to write *The Conspiracy,* a novel also influenced by his thoughts about the situation of writers in his own time.

This book takes an ingenious epistolary form of memoranda exchanged between Tigellinus, prefect (later commander) of the praetorian guard, and Paenus, tribune of the secret police, that often report verbatim intercepted letters between Lucan and Seneca. The basic story consists of these operatives' efforts to root out a conspiracy that has grown at least in part from their own paranoid imaginations as the emperor's courtiers. They reveal themselves whenever their communications depart from the circumspection of official prose, and in their meticulous transcription of the poets' correspondence Hersey develops remarkably complex characterizations of Lucan and Seneca. Both men are flawed as events begin drawing them toward their martyrdom. Lucan has never quite got over his early taste of imperial favor, and Seneca, comfortable in retirement, is vain and sententious. Lucan beseeches his uncle for advice about a writer's responsibilities, and Seneca, who should know why Lucan has posed the question, answers him almost as though a young man in Rome could emulate his bucolic detachment. "I see monstrosities, dear Seca," Lucan writes, "and it is not easy for me to keep myself close to my great work. The idea of art sometimes nauseates me when I think of what is happening in Rome in broad daylight. . . . What can a writer do?" (26–27). When Seneca replies that a writer's responsibility is to "avoid frenzy" because "this life . . . is not a proper basis for writing" (50), Lucan erupts:

I want to be *alive!* I am a poet. I do not wish to run until my body is warm. I want to exercise not my muscles but my senses until they are hot, hot, hot. My anger is at the center of my sanity. It goes out through my mouth, and I am purged and in good health.

Who said my *Pharsalia* is about the past? Not I. A writer is not responsible to the past, he must answer to the future. And therefore he cannot pretend that the present does not exist.(53)

The Roman present takes the form of an imperial gala planned by Tigellinus to offer matchless examples of every current pleasure, from a barge of amber and coral drawn by swans to a footrace of dwarfs and hunchbacks for a prize of copulation then and there with a volunteer noblewoman. Lucan's agonized reaction ("The faces of those poor creatures, Seca—devoid of any sense of their degradation" [81]) leads him to write Seneca again:

I know his [a writer's] duty is to his art—that he must stretch his gifts to the tearing point with every line he writes. But can there be a distinction, in times like these, between aesthetic achievement and vital action? You said that writers should stay away from power because they are forever wishing that reality could reach the level of art. I wonder, seeing reality so formless, so chaotic, so mad, whether this is not a reason why writers—artists in general—should not indeed approach very close to power through their works. (82)

Lucan becomes part of Piso's conspiracy by consenting to it when he realizes he cannot otherwise move Nero, who once spoke of being his muse. Lucan also recognizes that the police may be fomenting the plot, having been the first to imagine it. In the view of someone like Tigellinus, writers are eccentrics among the mass of subversives. Tigellinus sees only Lucan's vanity when he reads his questions about a writer's responsibility, and he is just clever enough to twist the meaning of the phrase and mock Lucan about his responsibilities when he is being interrogated. Hersey's subtlest effort in *The Conspiracy* comes in showing that Lucan can imagine writers becoming as the hunchbacks and dwarfs were in the footrace, "devoid of any sense of their degradation."

The eventual answer to Lucan's question is the obvious one that a writer writes, whether he avoids frenzy or courts it, whether his work is favored or proscribed. Hersey dramatizes this point in the deaths of nephew, uncle, and the indomitable Epicharis, mistress of Lucan's father. This guileless woman had long urged Lucan to visit his father's estate often enough to remain alive to nature and the sound of everyday life outside Rome. Under police interrogation, she states the plain truth of every circumstance and goes beyond merely truthful answers to observe in Nero's presence that he has been cruel in proscribing Lucan. When she hangs herself for fear of breaking under further torture and saying anything that might harm her husband or his son, the truth prevails by her action. A writer, Hersey implies, should attempt to do as well. Seneca, "rehearsed and ready," opens his veins in the company of friends to whom he delivers remarks on the pattern of his life. ("It is a man's bearing, as much as his words, that has real meaning," Paenus reports, consciously using Seneca's style [253].) In a last dictated message to Lucan, Seneca states that a writer must write; then he recalls that Lucan really wants to know what he can do about the evil in his world, and he rises to the truth he had evaded in an earlier letter to say that the writer must be among "those few men in every setting who try to find and live by the rules of wisdom; and who write down what little they learn" (254). Lucan faces his death without Epicharis's single-minded fortitude or Seneca's company of friends. Alone with Paenus and a physician, he weeps for his unfinished work and then begins reciting lines he has written for his hero Cato:

> What should be asked? Whether I'd rather die
> Free and armed, or swallow tyranny?
> Whether prolonging a life has any meaning,
> Or if years make a difference at all? Or whether a man,
> If he be good, can be hurt by any blow? (270)

He mumbles, whispers, and finally only moves his lips as he dies. It is left to Paenus, now Lucan's admirer and one envious of poets, to write, "The poem was all that was left alive in him" (270).

Hersey had himself been close to frenzy when he wrote *The Algiers Motel*

Incident and *Letter to the Alumni* in the years just before he went to Rome. He observed frenzies of protest and repression and braced himself at the edge of frenzy as he wrote. Although, obviously, never forbidden to publish, he could imagine Lucan's proscription keenly and feel how it would be exacerbated by spectacles in Nero's Rome.[21] *The Conspiracy* was written months after Hersey, in the closing pages of *Letter to the Alumni,* had described a possible future of repression in the United States. Although he drew no analogies between Nero's era and the present, Hersey wrote with the Nixon administration in mind and, necessarily, a steady reflection on a writer's responsibility as a citizen.[22] *The Conspiracy* is remarkable for *not* being didactic and for ending, in Lucan's death scene, with something other than Hersey's own recent example as a writer committed to social actions and public admonitions. The *Pharsalia* outlives the poet and is all he can give to the ongoing search for truth, the only testimony he can offer of his own search. In *The Conspiracy,* Hersey does not claim as much for the consequences of literary art as he does in his comments throughout the introduction and headnotes of his anthology *The Writer's Craft.* There, he admires Solzhenitsyn's proclaiming in *The First Circle* that "a great writer is, so to speak, a second government"[23] and praises Orwell's having "pushed art and morality together again, no matter how uncomfortably."[24] Would Hersey's dying Lucan, with "soundless rhythms" of *Pharsalia* on his lips, have agreed with the novelist-editor that "the final test of a work of art is not whether it has beauty, but whether it has power"[25] The point of Lucan's death scene seems to be that the beauty of his poem *is* its power—at least to the dying poet. That *The Conspiracy* can provoke such speculation makes it one of Hersey's most distinguished writings.

My Petition for More Space

The narrator of Hersey's short dystopian novel, *My Petition for More Space* (1974), is a writer. In some indefinite American future in which for two generations parents have been limited to one child, the narrator stands in a line of petitioners advancing four abreast for several blocks toward the business windows of a munipal building at which they will seek official approval for changes in various aspects of their highly regimented lives.

The narrator, Sam Poynter, is petitioning for more space, an increment from his current eleven-by-seven feet of sleeping quarters to the maximum individual allotment of twelve-by-eight feet, on the astonishing premise that he needs this space because he is a writer. He is little more than a clerk at the job in which his "shift of writers are due at the desklets," but he aspires to poetry and fiction. The man on his right in line would push him out for daring to make a request so outrageous that it would jeopardize everyone else's, and even the gentle young woman immediately ahead of him asks him whether he could not change his mind. "How can I change my mind," he reflects inwardly, "when my need underlies every choice, every action, every gesture of my life? . . . I am a writer. I need space" (104). When he finally reaches the windows that shield "mechanical voices" behind bars and opalescent glass, he cannot resist sarcasm and personal allusions that strike the window-voice as irrelevant, and he soon finds himself shouting that more space would give him more time. "A writer needs . . . ," he cries, in the last seconds at his disposal, only to have the voice finish the sentence with "nothing more than a bus driver."

There is little question about the story's outcome, because the fate of Sam Poynter's petition seals a parable expressing not so much future consequences of overpopulation as everyone's most familiar nightmares of overcrowding. In the petitioners' line there is no room to turn in any direction. Strict etiquette governs relations between "touchers," especially their sexual instincts. In domestic spaces, people do not move their possessions back and forth; they stack them and unstack them in place. Poynter does without television, lamps, rugs, or a desk, achieving a "highly personal style" by sacrificing possessions for space. Although the state makes most decisions once reserved to private citizens in less crowded societies, it is less conspicuous in this novel than the governments in *Nineteen Eighty-four* or *We*. The state appears only as the barred, frosted window at the head of the line. The fatuous voice behind it issues from a human being as mechanized as whatever collective mind and keyboard now print out notices from the Internal Revenue Service. There is no hint of Big Brother or of any ideology in this future New Haven (where Yale is never mentioned!). The only hint of revolution or imagination comes in Poynter's petition.

The action of *My Petition for More Space* is confined to Poynter's four-hour wait in line, and his point of view within that action is strictly limited to how far he can turn his head. Even his memories are cramped as they rise from his ever-narrowing world: "With my generation, on which proximity forced early visual intimacies, something strange happened: The eyes hardened. . . . And with the dulling of sight came a deadening of feeling, both in the fingertips and in the soul. I was perhaps a little different. This may be why I am special. I can still be surprised and thrilled by what I see. I am a writer. Powerful emotions are wired to my eyes. *This* is why I need space: I have to see sometimes at middle and long range" (107). *My Petition for More Space* might have been more moving if Poynter could have made that argument more powerfully, even to himself in the line, if not at the window, where no such petition would have had a chance. Beyond question, the novel succeeds in conveying the discomfort and frustration of its immediate setting. Discussing this novel, Hersey asked his interviewer to remember the ferry landing at Oak Cliffs where disembarking passengers could barely move in single file past people waiting four abreast to take their places aboard ship. With even more feeling, he then mentioned a recent photograph he had seen of a hundred thousand people on the beach at Peitaho in place of the two dozen that had usually been there during his childhood holidays from Tientsin.[26]

The Walnut Door

Condemned first for patronizing college students in *Too Far to Walk* and then for demonstrating "extravagances of the heart"[27] in their behalf in *Letter to the Alumni,* Hersey is ambivalent toward the dropout lovers in *The Walnut Door* (1977). He sympathizes with their efforts to live on their own at the same time that he satirizes the occasional self-indulgence in these efforts. He is playful in this novel, as he was in *Too Far to Walk* (more so in the exercise of his craft), yet at heart respectful enough of what had moved him at Pierson College to make some passages seem almost elegiac. If *The Walnut Door* should be the last of Hersey's books on contemporary education that begin with *The Child Buyer,* it is not a summing up but a backward glance at the aftermath of Mayday weekend 1970, a recognition that neither an American oppression nor a society of trust and decentralization that he had posed as alternate futures in *Letter to the Alumni* was coming to pass.

The jumpy present-tense narration of *The Walnut Door* places most events within the consciousness of Elaine, a young woman of precisely detailed background but no apparent occupation. Hersey was praised for the accuracy of undergraduate speech in *Too Far to Walk,* but here he shows more than a good ear. Elaine's talk rises above fidelity to her background to a toughness and chic that characterize her as someone on her own. The story begins as she moves into a lower-middle-class New Haven apartment in a "burrowing frame of mind" yet teased by the thought of "rebirth." This New Haven is almost as remote from Yale as the setting of *My Petition for More Space* is, as though Elaine and Eddie, her wily lover, had chosen to test their alienation from academic life by cultivating their indifference to it. Acquaintances may hang around the fringes of the campus, but the lovers come no closer than when Eddie chats with "a dignified gentleman in a gray sharkskin suit and porkpie hat . . . discreetly ransacking the barrels outside Davenport and Pierson colleges." (33) What the scavenger finds, in this ironic meeting of generations, could have been lost or discarded parts of the leftover possessions

Elaine brings to her new home. Her books are her "carton of assorted false starts," from *Utopia or Oblivion* by Buckminister Fuller through *The I Hate to Cook Book* by Peg Bracken and *Tristes Tropiques* by Claude Lévi-Strauss to *How to Get a Job Overseas* by Curtis Casewit. Elaine laps up the solicitude of a neighboring housewife who is "everything she dreaded becoming but could not help liking" (14) and ritually punishes her mother over the telephone. She appears to be courting a new existence as illusory as any old one when a telephone call abruptly changes her life. Eddie Macaboy is on the line, anonymously, for Safe-T Securit-E Syst-M, with his own survey and sales pitch for scaring young women living alone into buying stronger locks for their doors.

Macaboy sells locks in the hope of persuading customers to replace their doors; in his apartment, a small locksmith's shop is an antechamber to the carpenter's shop, which is the high altar of his life. He works in wood with the ease and love he could not cultivate when he was in college working with words, although Hersey obviously borrows from his own experience as a writer to describe Eddie's dedication. Macaboy makes a door with "none of your whorish bevels or molding, no panel freak's chamfers or astragals or bolections or cocked beads. Just one perfect surface on which the statements of nature will fill the eye, as they do in a seascape"—a vision that is the best proof of his claim he can "*think* all these things perfectly." (51) Elaine, coming off a disastrous long-term love affair, is wary of his every word and motion when he shows up at her apartment to install the lock, even as he makes a plausible case for replacing her flimsy door. Days later, he pries the door from the frame exactly as he warned her that it might happen and scatters her belongings—every token of her precious past except the photograph album that he steals—all over the floor and furniture. After a fearful interval, she orders the walnut door, which he installs with the deadbolt lock reversed, keyhole outward, locking her into her "dream" apartment.

This situation is confusingly resolved. Eddie, who has shown himself to be manipulative and a bit sneaky and who could even be held a criminal for some of his actions, has worked his apparent confidence game to draw his prisoner out of her "burrowing" and into a new life. He is the familiar hippie carpenter whose intentions are only a bit more flawed than the wood he chooses for his doors. Elaine apparently needs only to be locked in by such a man to set herself truly free. Captivity melts her halfheartedness, fears give way to exultation, and all suspicion of Eddie vanishes in rapturous fantasies:

Whatever this is, I have to give way to it, I have to let it happen to me. It was at first an airiness, the body active in it—beautiful long ground strokes all the way to the base line, easy and relaxed, an awareness that the game was expressing itself through her;

she was not the athlete but the instrument. The coolness in her yielded to a trembling flush. This was the first joy she had felt in months—perhaps ever—at least since childhood. *Light-years* away from any chemical high she had ever felt (189).

The novel ends with Eddie working on another door for another client.

Nancy L. Huse, in an appreciative and elaborate criticism of this novel, cites its "sharp, vibrant tone which seems to convey both pleasure and pain simultaneously."[28] This observation is particularly true of the language that records the skittery track of Elaine's mind. Harsh, witty, self-pitying, and self-mocking, she is brighter and more candid than Hester in *The Marmot Drive:* "Oh, God, they [her parents] explained and explained and explained; we had to see every split hair of right and wrong. They were so *boringly* decent. Dad was in love with our lab, Josephus. He was like St. Francis with that oaf of a hound. Mother, she was more of an amateur lawyer. What got her off was winning one for the good guys. She was always citing some decision of Justice Black or Learned Hand. They fell completely out of their tree over Stevenson" (79). In this passage Hersey almost manages to caricature his own generation along with Elaine's, softening the edges of the group portraits in *Letter to the Alumni*.

The Walnut Door is the strangest of the seven books Hersey wrote over the turbulent decade that began with his return to his alma mater. As apparently allegorical as *Under the Eye of the Storm,* it is not at all didactic. No story of Hersey's meanders as this one does in its short compass, and none ends as indefinitely.

Given the magnitude of his effort writing *The Call* over the next eight years and the wholly different outburst of fiction that followed, *The Walnut Door* may be Hersey's last word on Barry Rudd's generation.

Chapter Six
The Call: Homecoming

I have now determined that I will try to make a systematic search, through the
tangled nets of my memories, for whatever meaning I can find there—a
search, I presume, for the inner frame upon which the house of me stands.
    —*The Call,* 627 (David Treadup's introduction to "The Search.")

The Call (1985) is an extraordinary book.[1] Published after Hersey had
turned seventy, it is his most personal novel and his best. Few other American
novelists have had a life's work lead toward such a book, instead of seeing it
diminish in repeated disappointment.

The book is about an American missionary in China in the first half of the
twentieth century, but it may be read on at least two other levels beyond the
account of David Treadup's career. The missionary can stand for all Americans, altruists or adventurers or conscripts, who have offered the world their
dreams and talents. In his self-centered love of his work, this missionary also
resembles a novelist more than he does his typical colleague. However we see
David Treadup, he faces the meaning of existence more fully and finally than
any of Hersey's characters—even White Lotus or the survivors of Warsaw
and Hiroshima.

Like *The Wall,* this novel depends on Hersey's exhaustive historical research for facts and, in many senses, authority. As we have seen, the more
Hersey learned of the Warsaw ghetto, the more he was driven to invent the
"Levinson archive," his conscience leading him to create the authority he
lacked. In *The Call,* he felt no such inhibition. Generous quotation from
Treadup's writings (that is, creations of Hersey's drawn from the writings of
several missionaries) develops the protagonist's voice *within* a third-person
narration that gathers the momentum of judgment. This narration may be
Hersey's great technical achievement; it is certainly his subtlest. From the
opening tone of unobtrusive comment about passages in Treadup's diaries,
the narrator's authority grows to the point where his vision of the history that
often bewilders Treadup judges a man who would neglect his family in the
fury of his work and despair of his God when he was cut off from that work.

The Call is the culmination of Hersey's "Chinese" writings, of all the fiction and journalism he has produced about the country he often refers to as

his "natal land," and it is a revelation of how that body of work represents what is most persistent in his art and thought. The story of David Treadup's mission recalls the hope and disillusionment of the young American engineer in *A Single Pebble* at the same time that it reveals the limitations of both technology and American good intentions that Hersey has written about since his years as a war correspondent. The precise and evocative early twentieth-century Chinese setting of *The Call* is a sharp reminder of what Hersey tried to do in *White Lotus*, when he built a fable of racial identity from his own sense of being a foreigner as a child in Tientsin. In the historic China of *The Call* or the imagined Yellow Empire of *White Lotus*, readers will see that what they have taken, understandably, to be Hersey's preoccupation with the will to survive has become his questioning of the nature of existence.

In *The Call*, Hersey tries to re-create the world in which his father worked as an American Protestant missionary in China. As the writer put it in "Homecoming"—the record of his trip to Tientsin in 1981—he wanted to "find evidence that [his] parents' lives had been worth living." In these *New Yorker* articles Hersey describes how he had looked, sometimes with the help of someone who had known his parents, for traces that the YMCA's work in Tientsin had survived the revolution. How much any discovery meant to him may be judged by his reaction to news that Grace Hersey might have taught English to Zhou Enlai:

I stood at the front of the room and pictured my mother looking over Zhou's shoulder, helping him with an exercise, . . . not having any way in the world of knowing that she was teaching a boy who would one day be a great man. Maybe, by example, she was giving at least a little of her remarkable serenity to him. Mr. Huang had fixed 1914 as the year when this scene would have taken place. She was pregnant with me that year. I wanted to believe something of me had been in that classroom, too.[2]

The Call is the richly imagined record of the Chinese mission of David Treadup, an American YMCA secretary. Treadup's story is formed, in part, from those of six actual YMCA secretaries, including Roscoe Hersey, who would have been his contemporaries, but the novelist insists that his protagonist was not "like" any one of them. He may have been least like Roscoe Hersey, although details of Treadup's boyhood and especially of his being called to a foreign mission as a senior at Syracuse University are based on the elder Hersey's circumstances. Treadup in China is never like Roscoe Hersey, as John Hersey describes his father, bookish and "the gentlest of men." Treadup is ferocious. His books are the Bible and his diary. He is a writer more than a reader: keeping the diary, writing long letters back to the States, and copying into a commonplace book anything that might help him in his work. When interned by the Japanese, he begins writing "The Search," running through memories to find meaning in his life now that he has been taken from his beloved work. As John K. Fairbank remarked in his review of *The Call,* Treadup is "certainly the most articulate writer to have come out of the missionary movement."[3] Yet Treadup's writing is only one of the many outbursts of his energies. Roscoe Hersey worked hard, too, but one cannot imagine him in that work ever alienated from his wife and children, as Treadup is in his mission. Nor can one believe that, as illness forced his retirement, Roscoe Hersey could have felt forsaken by God and driven to apostasy, as Treadup felt in Japanese captivity. The novelist obviously drew upon the trials of his own vocation to portray Treadup's solitary labors and from doubts his father never expressed to make Treadup the existential figure he becomes.

As a boy in a meager upstate New York village, Treadup is raised as a typically purposeful and devout nineteenth-century American Christian. "Abracadabra!" his favorite teacher shouts before each classroom science demonstration, and Treadup believes ever after in the magic effect of such perfectly controlled performances. He grows increasingly confident that everything he learns, even the Latin course he is forced to repeat, will be applied to some great goal. At the turn of the century, he enters Syracuse University when the YMCA is at least as popular and powerful as the Greek-letter fraternities and offers, besides, in the Student Volunteer Movement a chance at public service that would not be approached on American campuses until the Peace Corps more than sixty years later. David, a rugged farm boy who strokes for the Orange crew and leads bonfire rallies, becomes converted to Christian service by three sentences spoken softly by an athlete-evangelist at a revival meeting: "Rejoice, O young man in thy youth" (Eccles. 11:9). "Remember now thy creator in the days of thy youth" (Eccles. 12:1). "For many are called but few are chosen" (Matt. 22:14). Hersey breaks from his narration to offer a sequence of four accounts of the experience taken from Treadup's writings. In "My Pledge," composed almost on the spot for no one else's eyes, the convert vows: "I, David Treadup, do of my own free will give myself, all that I am and have and will be, entirely unreservedly and unqualifiedly, to him, whom having not seen I love, in whom, though now I see him not, I believe." (66) In a letter to his parents soon afterward, he claims that "God crouching within [a classmate] spoke to me and told me that I must work for the rest of my life not for my interests but in his vineyard." (67) Five years later the moment is undiminished, as he writes from China to the Syracuse Christian Association: "[T]he miracle happened. I 'knew.' I saw a blinding light." (68) In "The Search," where Treadup is now writing as "a kind of apostate" in 1943, he insists that "the conversion was real," although he would "for the old phrase 'I found God' read 'I found myself.' In other words, the conversion was, in my case, a precipitate realization of my inner being." (69)

In so arranging these excerpts from Treadup's texts, Hersey confirms his hero's ardent self-centeredness and hints at his apostasy at this early stage of the novel. "Night after night," David writes his parents, "I played infinite variations upon a prayer of Benjamin Franklin's that particularly appealed to me: 'o powerful goodness! bountiful Father! merciful Guide! Increase in me that wisdom which discovers my true interests; strengthen my resolution to perform what that wisdom dictates.' " (66–67) The God revived for him on campus, even if unseen, offers him a life's work more completely his own than any he could hope to find in business or the professions. In his obsession with this fulfillment of his own "inner being," Treadup is more like a novelist than Noach Levinson, gathering items for his archive, is. Treadup resembles instead Lucan dying in *The Conspiracy* with only his poem alive in him at the last. Nothing illustrates the force of David's egotism better than his search for a wife once he is told that missionaries are expected to marry. References to Emily in his diary, then and ever afterward, are inseparable from trumpetings of his destiny, sometimes with unintended irony: "I love her! I believe that the greater the sacrifice for Jesus Christ, the greater the peace and satisfaction of life." (98) In the most moving scene of *The Call*—perhaps in all Hersey's writings—the author uses three points of view to describe David's first sight of Emily after their years of separation during World War II. (His diary has been blank for several months after this reunion, because "perhaps he could not bring himself to write honest words that might wound someone who happened to peek in his notebooks." [645]) Four years later, David would finally write in "Addendum to Search": "I was in health. I was useful. The clock and the calendar aren't necessarily reliable measurers of time. Here, before me, begging me with her eyes not to look at her, was an old woman. . . . What made it terribly hard was her being so afraid of my looking at her. Of course, I embraced her—partly, perhaps, to get her out of my field of vision—no! I loved her, I had promised myself an ecstasy" (645–46). ("Terrible, terrible!" Hersey said to me about Treadup's notations.)[4] Philip Treadup describes their parents' reunion to his brother Absolom: "The looks on their faces. You could tell he was trying not to look horrified, it certainly showed, and she was trying to look attractive. I thought, my God, he looks like one of her sons. . . . I just hope this animal doesn't crush what's left of poor Mother." (646–47)

When David arrives in China in 1905 he is disappointed to find himself living in foreign enclaves among missionaries who rationalize this segregation

as something the Chinese expect of them. The controversy over the nature of
the mission itself—whether to evangelize or spread the social gospel—has
come to a head and he is enmeshed in its contradictions. He yearns to win
souls for Christ as he himself had been converted, by appearing to have God
"crouching within him," but he is struck by the idea of giving science demonstrations ("So simple, yet how they can surprise") to his classes as a way of im-
pressing God's laws on their minds. He reads of the Jesuits' having sent men
especially trained in astronomy out to China so that they could humiliate
schools of Chinese astronomers by predicting the length and nature of the
eclipse of 1636. Suddenly David is inspired to lecture on the gyroscope as his
old high school teacher had done. Abracadabra! "I have a steel chain" he says
to audiences. "Can this chain stand up and walk? Can this chain run across
the room? Tell me . . . can this chain climb that ladder over there?" (214–
15). And geared to a wheel, the chain, a "wrestling gyroscope," does all these
things. Treadup seems neither an evangelist nor a social worker as he contem-
plates this stage of his mission:

There is for me in science a marvelous beauty, a great exultation, an inexpressible enthusiasm that makes these experiences seem priceless, and I have a great yearning
that each of my friends in the audience shall also experience the thrilled yet calm certainty that this beauty makes me feel. I want to fill them with a sense of power, a
sense of victory, and a sense of potentiality. This emotional and dramatic experience
that they go through with me makes a deep and abiding impression upon them.
They can carry it away and can go on remembering and thinking about it, both consciously and unconsciously, long afterward. This is of great moment for the future of
China (217–18).

Does he set his chain in motion to serve the needs of the Chinese people, to
convert them to Christianity, or to feed his unappeasable energies? "I am ad-
dicted to applause," he writes, in one of his hurried acknowledgments of self-
doubt; "I need more and more" (282).

Treadup reaches China in the last, faltering years of the Manchu dynasty,
when every major power except the United States had attempted to wrest
some concession of Chinese soil. While Chinese appreciation of this forbear-
ance had not spared all American missionaries from martyrdom, Treadup
and his countrymen had brighter opportunity than their European colleagues
with reform-minded Chinese by "using gravity," letting their ideas and
"wrestling gyroscopes" first impress the most influential persons at hand, but
even as they used "gravity," the Americans could do no more than listen to
dire predictions for China upon the accession of the three-year-old Pu Yi to

the imperial throne and be ignorant of any hint that the dynasty would be overthrown. The civil war breaking out is noise and confusion to Treadup as he boards a train in Peking. Revolution catches him by surprise, "his absorbed mind cut off from the obvious reality" (232). Treadup will interview Sun Yat-sen and be led by Sun's apparent pro-American bias to hope "for a China that would both be Christian and be an aspiring replica of his [Treadup's] homeland in its customs and institutions" (239–40). Treadup's mission unfolds in the years that Professor Fairbank has called the interregnum between the Manchus and Mao,[5] when the warlords rise and fall, the Kuomintang emerges within the beleaguered republic, the Communists regroup and retreat after their rupture with the Kuomintang, and the Japanese invade in force. On his lecture tours Treadup meets most of the major reformers and aspiring political leaders before they have either failed or gained power: Sun, Chiang, and Mao; Yuan Shih-k'ai, dissident in the empire; the "Christian" General Feng; and Liang Ch'i-Ch'ao, author of *The New Citizen,* for a while Mao's bible. Hersey, through his narrator, passes from exuberant notations in Treadup's papers first to observe that the lecturer was probably unaware of the potential importance of these men (except as YMCA supporters) and then to make a historical judgment that Treadup did not live to venture: "Yuan turned out to be a powermonger, Liang a conservative. Feng finally not a Christian but a Communist sympathizer, Sun a disappointment, Chiang a reactionary, and Mao a Marxist emperor. But all of that was to be a long, sad story for the unfolding future, and at the moment of the handshakes after the Treadup lecture on flying machines, wonderful things— great marvels in China!—seemed altogether possible" (264).

Obsessed with his work, Treadup turns vain in his obsession and blind alike to political reality and criticism of his mission. A colleague is shot before his eyes and the civil war leads to his family's evacuation, but Treadup roars about the countryside on his Indian motorcycle and writes to his ancient YMCA rival, James Todd, a fierce representative of its evangelical wing: *"The darker the political situation is, the keener is the realization on the part of thinking people of the urgency and importance of uplifting the masses. We are going great guns. This is one of the strange phenomena of this country that puzzles foreigners who daily read such headlines as WAR, OPIUM, ROBBERY ect. [sic] They cannot understand how constructive forces can be operating while political chaos seems to be the order of the day. But they are, thank God!"* (398). Evangelists in China write Todd to urge Treadup's removal for being a godless modernist lecturer, while other enemies accuse him of consorting with Communists. In his neglect of the Word, Treadup is condemned as a humanist. His reaction is to mollify his critics so that he can stay in China, but there is no hint of his seeing any truth in the near-hysterical charges. He is obviously a humanist, and the YMCA has in him an unflagging force for social betterment, even at the expense of his family when his stipends are reduced and finally cut off during the depression, and he is forced to beg support from a Chinese patron. He works in remote villages, "living Chinese" even before his wife has been sent home to America. If anything keeps Treadup's mission from becoming godless at that point, it is his furious writing to those he has left in the world outside the villages, and that is the overflow, as well as the record, of his obsession.

Even before internment, Treadup may have gained some sense of being overtaken by history. The reader can never be more certain about this point than the narrator, who has gathered from Treadup's writings and from outside sources only the knowledge that the missionary met with a team of four Communists who had been indoctrinating nearby peasants on issues of the "patriotic war against Japan," and that he had been surprised to find himself arguing with them. One learns that the team considered the missionary an imperialist propagandist and demanded his removal; then that the villagers refused to take this action and insisted upon the meeting instead. Treadup is typically effusive in his diary entry the day before: *"I am going to go on working for the well-being of the peasants in these villages, whether the team likes it or not. If it comes to a showdown, they'll find that the villagers will choose me over them. I shall tell them to keep out of the twelve villages, at least for a few months—let it be a separate little province"* (550). But of the meeting itself there is not a word in his hand except for lines in "The Search" recalling the heat, not the substance, of an argument. It was an "astonishing and unnatural silence," the narrator observes. "On everything he records from then on, there is a faint but permanent stain, a toxic trace, an imprint of some kind of foreboding" (550), and the reader is suddenly left to question how much this impression marks what he has read of "The Search."

Treadup's unrecorded meeting with the Communists appears to have been even more decisive in his mission than the termination of that mission by the Japanese. Everything that he had understood up to then had come to him as a revelation of God's laws, followed by an eager deduction of how those laws might be applied for man's benefit. Suddenly he either was utterly bewildered or first entertained doubts about the success of his mission. Whatever happened did not keep Treadup from returning to China in 1946 for secular relief efforts that he stuck to until the triumphant Communists packed him off back to the United States. He did not despair immediately after the interview in either a conventional or an existential sense. He may have turned silent because he had no words for the enormity of a political theory that seemed to have reached these Communist circuit riders with as much force as God's word was spoken to him at Syracuse or for a political program that functioned for these young Chinese as reassuringly as God's laws and their applications had for him. Treadup's unutterable perception of this meeting may have been that the Communists' mission was superseding his.

There are two phases to Treadup's internment. For the first fifteen months after Pearl Harbor, he is under house arrest in Tientsin; from 15 March to 23 August 1943, he is in a concentration camp, until the Japanese repatriate a large group of American missionaries. The first phase is marked by voracious reading under the direction of his skeptical friend Dr. Cunningham, to enable him, in his tutor's phrase, to "enter the twentieth century." He begins with *Don Quixote* soon after writing in his diary: *"I might never again see roses bloom on the arbor I built to celebrate my love for my wife and sons. Worse than that, far worse than that. The bottom had dropped out from under my useful life. My entire life for Christ had been wasted. Lectures! Where had they led? The villages!—hollow shells. Everything I had done had been swallowed up into absurdity"* (573). Reading Montaigne's essays side by side with Emerson's, then *Moby-Dick,* Spinoza, and Nietzsche, Treadup writes of a strange homesickness, not any home he had made with Emily but for his villages at Ma Ch'iao, and with it "a deep, deep nostalgia for a sense of worth." The Japanese make off with his gyroscope—which is his symbol as much as a cross would be to another missionary—that he had kept close by since his science-teaching demonstrations.

In the camp, he notes in his diary a long night, near hallucination, pacing his room and arguing with the imagined voices of several friends, that leads to a confused notation that he is *"out of touch with God. It may be that I realized that night—that I now think—that there is no God. On that point I am not sure"* (619). Soon afterward he begins to write "The Search." The essay is to be *"a systematic search, through the tangled nets of my memories, for whatever meaning I can find there—a search, I presume, for the inner frame upon which the house of me stands"* (627). By the time the reader learns of these intentions, segments of "The Search" have become an integral part of the novel, Treadup's driven memories accompanying his fervent diary entries and challenging what the narrator has surmised. Had Hersey used "The Search" as an appendix, as he once considered doing, he would have lost much of the tension in his story and seriously weakened his characterization of Treadup. It is this portrait of the man given over to his work and devastated by losing it that raises Treadup above all other characters in Hersey's fiction.

Of all Hersey's novels about twentieth-century events, *The Call* is the least likely to be disparaged as "fictionalized journalism," a phrase that presumably applies better to such a topical novel as *A Bell for Adano*. Even in his most admired earlier books, *Hiroshima* and *The Wall,* the burden of what Hersey perceived as his obligation to his subject led him to artistic choices that provoked the harshest comments these books have received. Hersey has been attacked for understating the horror of the Hiroshima bombing. As Kingsley Widmer put it, "artful detail substitutes for moral intelligence."[6] *The Wall* has been described by Frederic Karl as "inert . . . history at the expense of its novelistic elements."[7] Whatever the justice of such criticism, we do know why Hersey deliberately chose to be impersonal in *Hiroshima* and, in much greater detail, his belief that he lacked the authority to be even the conventional narrator of his story of the Warsaw ghetto. By contrast, *The Call* is a genuine "novel of contemporary history," unquestionably stirred by events in Treadup's mission (and in Hersey's background) but always taking those events as signs of a historical significance encompassing that mission. The special distinction of *The Call* beyond all its differences with Hersey's other books may be Hersey's presence as the narrator and the compiler of Treadup's archive, revealing much of himself in unfolding Treadup's obsession. Searching for traces of his parents' work in Tientsin in 1981, Hersey would soon deliver the largest of these traces in the completed manuscript of this novel.

Chapter Seven
Blues and Later Stories

Just as he had rushed into many possibilities of fiction in the early fifties after finishing *The Wall,* Hersey went from eight years' writing of *The Call* to a new string of short stories and *Blues,* a book of imaginary conversations on the subject of angling for bluefish off Martha's Vineyard. (As the present study of his work goes to press, he is writing a novel.[1]) *The Call,* which appeared to close a circle of Hersey's writings about China, has opened another swift freshet of fiction and in "God's Typhoon" even a story set in Peitaho about a missionary's child. His only reporting assignment during these years[2]—the 1987 meeting in Moscow of the International Physicians for the Prevention of Nuclear War—has not carried over into his other work, and at this writing it is too soon to expect stories shaped by the events of 1989—even a response to his anguish over the suppression of students at Tiananmen Square. Instead, Hersey's new fiction deals with Americans close at hand—those he lived among in the Northeast in the later twentieth century. A satirical streak flashes through the ample variety of this fiction from Fisherman's understatement in *Blues* to the lavishly developed character of the narrator of "Fling."

Blues

"Good and honorable recreations are the cause of man's fair old age and long life," Dame Juliana Berners wrote in *Treatise of Fishing with an Angle* (1496), which Hersey cites as the original example of the "high moral line" taken by writers on fishing (*Blues,* 104–5). The line suits him well in *Blues,* almost as though he were playing out and reeling in the didacticism with which he is often charged. In a dozen conversations between Fisherman and Stranger, the writer digresses easily from instruction in bluefishing to meditations on the fish's place and his own in the chains of life surrounding them on the Middle Ground outside Vineyard Haven.

The form of *Blues* varies slightly from the conversations between Piscator and Venator in Izaak Walton's *Compleat Angler* (1653). All of Walton's flowing talk comes in one glorious but typical day of fishing (a fiction that leaps hearteningly over credibility). Hersey attempts a more dramatic structure of twelve trips out in his boat, *Spray,* over the course of a season of bluefish from 10 June to 28 October. There is a subtle difference between the fishing partnerships in the two books. Whereas Venator is won over at once to Piscator's claims for the preeminence of angling among all recreations, Stranger, even after he becomes devoted to bluefishing, will occasionally disagree with Fisherman's pronouncements and catch him in contradictions. The pattern of conversation in *Blues* provides, as one might expect of dialogue by a novelist, more of a narrative than can be found in *The Compleat Angler.* (But *The Compleat Angler* offers *far* more practical fishing instruction than *Blues* does.) Stranger is initiated quickly, and the discourses on the environment begin with Fisherman's explanation of why they must keep no more fish than they need for the table that night. Stranger, who had been averse to fishing because he considered it a blood sport, begins to understand the environment once his natural rapacity as a fisherman has been aroused.

The particular grace of *Blues* lies in Hersey's doing justice to his reflections without diminishing his celebration of the sport. Stranger acknowledges this quality by noticing his host's complex responses to their outings: delight and discomfort, exhilaration and foreboding, Fisherman's "warning against applying human terms and values to fishes yet doing it all the time" (106). Thus, Fisherman is all for saving the tern at the expense of the predator herring gull, which he hates; he wonders at the never-observed sex habits of bluefish and notes that fish and fishing have always been associated with sex. Each conversation ends with a recipe for preparing bluefish, Stranger's hearty compliments to the chef, and a poem that Fisherman has thought of at sea and promised to look up in his library. "I'll never get enough of the sea. . . . I dream of the wonders I'll never lay eyes on," Fisherman exclaims, and rolling from the crest of such happiness he confesses that "fishing has made me face myself as a member of my careless species" (173).

Walton walked out Tottenham Court Road to fish clear streams before the age of factories. Each day's fishing reminded him "that *the meek possess the earth;* or rather, they injoy what the other possess and injoy not; for Anglers and meek quiet-spirited men, are free from those high, those restless thoughts which corrode the sweets of life." Fishing was revelation: "So when I would beget *content,* and increase confidence in the *Power,* and *Wisdom,* and *Providence* of Almighty God, I will walk the *Meadows* by some gliding stream, and there contemplate the *Lillies* that take no care, and those very many other various little living *creatures* that are not onely created but fed (man knowes not how) by the goodness of the God *of Nature.*"[3] Hersey, in a grimmer time, is always conscious of his species "meddling dangerously in the affairs of a vast organism." No study or contemplation of fishing and the sea is immune from that meddling, whether on a rare day when one may look down to the shoal of the Middle Ground or at the Woods Hole laboratories where an arsonist once destroyed a holding tank of bluefish. Fisherman runs to the limit of chains of being and then reverses himself: "I'm caught on an invisible line, and I'm being pulled toward a fish."

Later Stories

Fling and *Other Stories* (1990), Hersey's first story collection, contains only two of his efforts from the early postwar years: the rollicking "Peggety's Parcel of Shortcomings" and the bitter encounter of two American colonels in China, "Why Were You Sent Out Here?" The remaining nine have all appeared in astonishingly rapid succession since 1987 in magazines as varied as *Yale Review* and *The Yacht.* "The Terrorist" is the only one of these stories remotely tied to events since 1987, but it is less about terrorism than about perception of terrorism through the mass media—specifically, terrorism displayed in a four-panel comic strip. Several others are set in pockets of the recent past underrepresented in Hersey's previous work: times that may be central to the story as the depression is in "Mr. Quintillian" or more often peripheral as the accession of John F. Kennedy is in the title story and "The Announcement."

Domestic behavior is the most common subject in these stories, and because of this they are more subtly satirical than such earlier works as *The Child Buyer.* Hersey's observations in these stories reminded one reviewer of Jane Austen's,[4] and the Thanksgiving table in "The Announcement," in illustrating this similarity, shows how much more Hersey delivers in almost any scene or situation of his later fiction than he did in "Why Were You Sent Our Here?" or "The Pen" or even the delight of Peggety's monologue. In "The Announcement" nothing upsets the sudden affinity between the narrator's fiancée and his mother: not political arguments, sibling sniping, a spilled glass, the narrator's untimely toast to the two women he loves, or their own surprise in discovering each other's warmth.

Some measure of Hersey's later craft may come from seeing how "Requiescat" improves on a similar idea in the earlier "The Death of Buchan Walsh." In both stories, the narrator gives up his attempt to write about a friend whose character he cannot quite define. Hersey relied on ingenuity in "The Death of Buchan Walsh" by having the writer observe his friend in a situation contrived to resemble one he cannot resolve in a story he is writing about him. In "Requiescat" the narrator begins by thinking of himself as Moose Bradford's one true mourner qualified to write a honest memoir. The upshot of the situation in "The Death of Buchan Walsh" is that life neither imitates the notes the writer has for his next episode nor provides anything better in their place. What the writer learns years later of Buchan's death in World War II reveals a mystifying inertia at the core of his friend's character—unfortunately, nothing he is inclined to write about. Hersey concentrates the action of "Requiescat" into interviews and researches that culminate with an FBI file gained under the Freedom of Information Act, for the writer's friend had gone to prison briefly while a defense attorney at congressional hearings in the McCarthy era. What the writer has learned suddenly clarifies his one unclear memory of Moose Bradford, and he tosses what he has written into the apartment refuse chute—"from which there was no return"—along with any thought of pursuing the project. From the blocked writer of "The Death of Buchan Walsh," Hersey has come up with a wiser man who must bury his friend rather than praise him.

"God's Typhoon" is quite unlike anything else that reaches into Hersey's Chinese childhood. The narrator recalls a summer in his childhood at Peitaho, "the heavenly enclave on Chinese soil where Chinese were unwelcome," while warlords ravaged North China and a British submarine surfaced offshore. Like Hersey, the narrator was the younger child in an American missionary family making believe within the compound while his older brothers were off on serious errands. His story follows no one actual incident but, rather, bears traces of Hersey's research for *The Call*. While it does not illuminate the writer's loss of religious belief, it does offer some of the vivid horrors and insights that could give a missionary child a background for that loss.

Dr. Wyman, the boy's next-door neighbor, is the most robust type of muscular Christian, a preacher of interminable, terrifying sermons. He is a soul saver of "prodigious mental and physical gifts." A giant of a man like David Treadup, he is also profoundly curious about God's natural laws, cluttering his summer house with tools and instruments and keeping an arboretum nearby in which he has planted every conifer that could survive in the temperate zone of North China. Unlike Treadup, he hoards all this scientific passion for his own amusement and closes his arboretum to visitors. His own son, the narrator's playmate, is mortally afraid of him and becomes torn between that fear and the temptations conceived by his high-spirited friend. One night the boys pitch their pup tent inside the forbidden grove and are awakened by Dr. Wyman's uprooting the tent by its ridgepole and shouting imprecations at them, as he chases them from this garden for their blatant display of original sin (the narrator had brought matches along, to Dr. Wyman's particular horror: "You brought flame into my arboretum . . . , you little devil"). The boys may take Dr. Wyman as an image of God. To the narrator he personifies the angry God he preaches, but at least from the distance of the house next door. The reader must imagine, from the boy's cowering behavior, how much more he terrifies his own son.

The next afternoon, twisters of a typhoon descend on the enclave, battering houses, uprooting every tree in the arboretum, and killing Dr. Wyman. The narrator experiences "a surge of the greatest joy" he has ever known, because God had spoken to him in the roar of the typhoon, forgiving him and punishing the wrathful master of the arboretum. But the joy vanishes when he learns that Dr. Wyman was killed because he had gone out in the storm looking for his son. The focus of the story then turns, at its conclusion, upon the fearful neighbor boy, who takes up his father's burdens by overseeing the first replanting of the arboretum.

What the child understood of the typhoon after his playmate returned from mourning is not disclosed, nor does the adult narrator betray any meaning that may have come to him over the years. This reticence is extraordinary, not merely after the morals pointed and asserted in Hersey's stories but especially coming in the aftermath of the effort than went into David Treadup's "Search." If this story is based, however remotely, on something that actually happened to Hersey, all it reveals of that occurrence is the "scaredness" and "sacredness" that, as he writes in *Blues* (102), often come to him out on the sea in *Spray*.

The old woman who tells her story in "Fling" will strike many of Hersey's readers as being uncannily oblivious to almost all the historic matters of her time. The great exception is the emergence of "the coloreds," whom she can deal with as individuals but not in threatening masses. Yet even a friendly waiter can lead her to wonder what it would be like if "they" were doing the tipping. They are on the edge of her reminiscence, however, for she is about to go abroad for the last time, on foot across a bridge to Ciudad Juarez. She is dying at seventy-nine, a relic in the first year of "our boy president, Jack Kennedy" from times that Hersey, missionary's child and scholarship student, knew at fairly remote second hand. Venus (nicknamed from an ancient "skinny-dipping" episode in which she emerged surprised from the surf) notes that she was often unfaithful in the same breath that she can dismiss her grandson because "his principal extracurricular activity was getting filthy." But Hersey does not imply that she is a hypocrite; she and her handsome husband have traveled through most of the twentieth century à trois, even à cinc ("there's always a floater, so to speak"), and at the end that floater is simply

death or, in the narrator's phrase, the Topic. As her narration becomes less coherent, Hersey changes to an external point of view in which Venus, with faltering steps, "looks like the ghost of a pirate" just before she collapses. As *The
Call* is the culmination of Hersey's novels, so this story is the peak of his restless diversions in short fiction.

Chapter Eight

A Writer's Craft

"The final test of a work of art is not whether it has beauty," Hersey states in the introduction to his anthology *The Writer's Craft,* "but whether it has power."[1] How writers achieve this power eludes succinct description in Hersey's comments accompanying the statements about writing that he has gathered from three poets, a critic (Percy Lubbock), and twenty-eight writers of fiction. These writers examine hundreds of practices of their craft that they find in their work, and many of them also try to understand what they do before they get to the writing itself—"back-of-the-head work," Hersey calls it, in *Blues* and elsewhere. From both kinds of self-scrutiny, one gathers that power tests craft and that craft is the upshot of a struggle between forces Hersey represents as "supplier" and "censor," elements of the writer's unconscious and conscious minds.

George Orwell and Alexander Solzhenitsyn, among Hersey's sources, write most emphatically of an urgency that acts upon both supplier and censor. Hersey's headnote to Solzhenitsyn's Nobel Lecture summarizes the years the Russian writer spent imprisoned and then proscribed before the Nobel award in 1970, as if to explain Solzhenitsyn's special qualifications for lecturing on the theme of the artist's responsibility. Solzhenitsyn could remark, in *The First Circle,* that the great writer is a "second government" because before anyone else suspected his own greatness Solzhenitsyn had been such a government within the gulag of the Soviet state. In him and in Orwell, urgency made the struggle between supplier and censor a furious collaboration. Their writings are obviously tested by their power more than by any consideration of their beauty. The other contents of *The Writer's Craft* refer more to Hersey's inquiries as a writing teacher in 1974, such as "the whole intricate question of method"—matters that had concerned him passionately, even at urgent moments during World War II. What we make of Hersey's lifework begins with our understanding both his earnest approach to the world and his adventurous spirit in his craft.

Hersey, first to last, has dealt seriously with important subjects.[2] When he was a war correspondent, this writing was severely circumscribed by events themselves and the state of mind called "the war effort." Most civilians

Hersey's age postponed the mastery of their crafts for the duration of the war, while the writer, blessed or damned by circumstance, began practicing his aboard the *Hornet* and on Guadalcanal. When Hersey proceeded from reporting events as they occurred—from attempting clear exposition of what he had seen—he was limited in his freedom to interpret their meaning. In *Into the Valley,* Americans fight the war "to get it over with" and get home. Accuracy of detail and the spatial or narrative arrangement of accurate detail in Hersey's dispatches imply far more meaning than such wartime think pieces as "Experience by Battle" convey.

Fiction had seemed a way of saying more about events than Hersey could report in dispatches when he attempted a novella about carrier pilots he met aboard the *Hornet.* When events in the Sicilian campaign led him to think about the reconstruction of society in the postwar world, Hersey returned to fiction and wrote *A Bell for Adano* "at white heat" and with marked facility. His reputation ever since has been haunted by this highly readable and widely read tale. The rest of his novels have been more complex, and a few have been more obscure; some reviewers in 1944 claimed that he oversimplified his ideas, and some literary historians have dismissed, rather cursorily, what they perceive as his "fictionalized journalism." The grain of truth in these opinions is that the urgency of events, the burden of what he had seen and heard, gripped Hersey in the weeks that he wrote *A Bell for Adano,* as it would, much more oppressively, in the years that he worked on *The Wall.* He was a novelist of these events more than he could be a novelist of the ideas that issued from them. His urgency could work in strange ways on other occasions. As the reporter assembling the testimony of Hiroshima survivors, he built a narrative upon the example of Thornton Wilder's structure in *The Bridge of San Luis Rey*—"fictionalizing" journalism in a way almost unnoticed among praises of his response to an urgent occasion.

The Wall, much more than *Hiroshima* or *A Bell for Adano,* shows Hersey writing in the agony of a specific responsibility. He "did not know," but he "could have known," he said much later, what Benjamin Weintraub told him at Klooga, what "Alfred Stirmer" and ghetto documents read by his translators told him later. This knowledge made him self-effacing in a way perilous for novelists when he created Levinson to exercise authority that he himself felt powerless to assume as narrator, and even Levinson "narrates" within his activity of compiling an archive. Distinguishing between journalism and fiction, Hersey has written that a journalist must know, while a novelist has freedom to invent. The three books for which he is still best known show how far he could go to the limits of reporting and how that venturing affected his early growth as a writer of fiction.

The first four novels after *The Wall* belong to a decade in which Hersey was devoted to what he called "the possibilities of fiction." With varying success, these books take up ideas more than actual events embodying those ideas. *A Single Pebble,* for example, presents the impact of Western technology on an ancient culture in the story of the American engineer who travels up the Yangtze sometime in the century's early twenties and his own, as deliberately vague a period as Hersey can establish for his idea. *The Marmot Drive,* on the other hand, is a moral tale that begs to be read as an allegory of events rather than of ideas. *The War Lover* contrasts two men and the ideas they represent, with little reference to specific events in their war. *The Child Buyer* does indeed react to the present state of its subject but does so in satire that is rarely topical. *A Single Pebble* is Hersey's first book about China, a foreshadowing of *The Call,* and, as we can now see, the beginning of self-exploration in his fiction. *The War Lover* may be taken as his last word on World War II, particularly on the theme of combat. *The Child Buyer* is the first of several books touching the problems of bright students in a democratic education. These books, for all their variety of ideas and technique, were indifferently reviewed when they appeared—except for the arguments on education provoked by *The Child Buyer*—and Hersey by 1960 had gained far less attention as a postwar novelist than he had for his writing on Hiroshima and the Warsaw ghetto.

White Lotus may be Hersey's most ambitious work. Certainly the heroine's narrative is his most intricate fictional creation. But the reception of this book was disappointing in many ways. It was read almost exclusively as a topical allegory. It did not clarify anyone's effort to describe the variety of his work; that variety seemed instead a miscellany beside the apparent sequences of growth in the books of some of his contemporaries. *White Lotus* did not, like Bellow's *Herzog,* appear to range further within familiar preoccupations or advance an established style or, like some of Cheever's fiction at this time, make the essence of the author's talent more conspicuous. *White Lotus* lacked humor at a time when it was being compared unfavorably to *Invisible Man* and when, moreover, humor was being discovered in almost every other American novelist with a claim to significance.

Between *White Lotus* and *The Call,* Hersey wrote five other novels that are at least as discrete as the five from *The Marmot Drive* to *White Lotus.* He also returned to journalism dramatically, with *The Algiers Motel Incident,* a montage of interviews that contrasts fascinatingly with *Hiroshima.* From 1965 to 1970, at the height of the student movement, he was Master of Pierson College, and he went on to teach at Yale throughout the seventies. He became a critic, partly from teaching, with his commentary in *The Writer's Craft* and his essay on a recurrent topic in his seminars: the distinctions between journal-ism and fiction. In 1977 he began research for *The Call*. Although his novels of these two decades were noticed even less than his fiction in the fifties was, they include two of his best, *Under the Eye of the Storm* and *The Conspiracy*. These books demonstrate that he is not, as I suggested twenty-five years ago, "something other than a novelist" but, rather, an accomplished novelist of ideas. In these books he refines his methods of discussing serious ideas within a well-constructed story. The hero of *Under the Eye of the Storm* keeps his yawl afloat through a line storm that develops suspense simultaneously with an ar-gument against excessive technology in man's struggle with nature. "But the whole point is being out *in* it, getting through it," Tom Medlar shouts. In *The Conspiracy*, Hersey makes fiction of history from several ancient sources to develop ideas of a writer's responsibility. When Lucan dies with his poem on his lips, has power been tested or beauty? "Avoid frenzy," Seneca advises him; "a writer must write." But Seneca, retired in the country, can avoid frenzy, while Lucan, proscribed in Nero's Rome, cannot.

Most reviews of *The Call* praised Hersey's mastery of his material without discussing the book in relation to his other work. Reviewers were moved by the story of David Treadup, and some noted references to the novelist's father as a minor character (Treadup's colleague in Tientsin), without commenting on how his appearance was a possible reflection of Hersey's own presence in this book. Hersey's narration encompasses Treadup's own vivid accounts of his experiences, its subtle tone moving from dispassionate commentary to judgment. It is Hersey's most accomplished display of his "voice" in all of his writing, whether in any of his delegated narrations or in his admiring essays on survivors. *The Call* is powerful beyond Hersey's other work because its hero, always in the narrator's view, comes closer than any of the writer's other fictional or actual subjects to questioning the meaning of existence.

The quality that makes *The Call* Hersey's best work is expressed by Tolstoy in a passage Hersey reprints in *The Writer's Craft:* "Speech transmit-ting the thoughts and experiences of men serves as a means of union among them, and art serves a similar purpose. The peculiarity of this latter means of intercourse, distinguishing it from intercourse by means of words, consists in this, that whereas by words a man transmits his thoughts to another, by art he transmits his feelings to another."

Notes and References

Chapter One

1. "The Legend on the License," *Yale Review* 20, no. 5 (Autumn 1980): 2.
2. Hersey's statement in *Current Biography* (New York: Wilson, 1944), 286.
3. See "My First Job," *Yale Review* 76, no. 2 (Winter 1987): 183–97, and Mark Schorer, *Sinclair Lewis: An American Life* (New York: McGraw-Hill, 1961), 631.
4. W. A. Swanberg, *Luce and His Empire* (New York: Scribner, 1972), 207.
5. "Henry Luce's China Dream," *New Republic,* 2 May 1983, 27.
6. Ibid., 29.
7. Theodore White, *In Search of History: A Personal Narrative* (New York: Harper & Row, 1978), 84.
8. "Joe Grew, Ambassador to Japan," *Life,* 15 July 1940, 77–83.
9. Interview with the author, Vineyard Haven, Massachusetts, 13 August 1987.
10. *Men on Bataan* (New York: Knopf, 1942), 23. Further page references to Hersey's books appear in parentheses and are to Knopf editions.
11. Fletcher Pratt, "The Epic of Bataan," *Saturday Review of Literature,* 4 June 1942, 20; "Hero as an Army," *Time,* 1 June 1942, 80.
12. "Nine Men on a Four Man Raft," *Life* 2 November 1942, 54–57.
13. "Experience by Battle," *Life,* 27 December 1943, 51.
14. Interview with the author, 13 August 1987.
15. See Philip Knightley, *The First Casualty: From the Crimea to Vietnam: The War Correspondent as Hero, Propagandist, and Myth Maker* (New York: Harcourt, Brace, Jovanovich, 1975), 275–302.
16. Interview with the author, 13 August 1987.
17. Ibid.
18. Ibid.
19. Samuel B. Girgus, "Against the Grain: The Achievement of John Hersey," Ph.D. diss., University of New Mexico, 1972, 23–26.
20. Henry R. Luce, "The American Century," *Life,* 16 February 1941, 61.
21. "AMGOT at Work," *Life,* 23 August 1943, 29.
22. Orville Prescott, "Books of the Times," *New York Times,* 7 February 1944, 11; Diana Trilling, "Fiction in Review," *Nation,* 12 February 1944, 194–95.
23. Except as noted, details in this paragraph are from interview with the author, 13 August 1987.

24. Jonathan Dee, "The Art of Fiction, XCII. John Hersey," *Paris Review* 100 (Summer/Fall 1986): 216.

25. J. Donald Adams, "Speaking of Books," *New York Times Book Review*, 7 May 1944, 2.

26. "Engineers of the Soul," *Time*, 9 October 1944, 99.

27. "Days, Nights, and a Few Years," *New Yorker*, 3 November 1945, 90.

28. Dwight Macdonald, "Hersey's 'Hiroshima,' " *Politics* 3 (October 1946): 308.

29. Tom Wolfe, *The New Journalism* (New York: Harper & Row, 1973), 45–46; Mas'ud Zavarzadeh, *The Mythopoeic Reality: The Postwar American Nonfiction Novel* (Urbana: University of Illinois Press, 1976), 94.

30. Dee, "The Art of Fiction, XCII. John Hersey," 225.

31. Whittaker Chambers, *Witness* (New York: Random House, 1952), 498.

32. "A Reporter at Large. The Communization of Crow Village," *New Yorker*, 27 July 1946, 38.

33. "Red Pepper Village," *Life*, 26 August 1946, 92.

34. "A Reporter in China. Two Weeks' Water Away," *New Yorker*, 18 May 1946, 59–69; 25 May 1946, 54–69.

35. Dee, 226. Other details in this paragraph are from interview with the author, 13 August 1987.

36. See Frederick R. Karl, *American Fictions, 1940–1980* (New York: Harper & Row, 1983), 586.

37. Ibid.

38. A summary of this reaction can be found in the *New York Times Book Review*, 10 November 1946, 7.

39. Michael Yavenditti, "John Hersey and the American Conscience," *Pacific Historical Review* 43 (February 1974): 48.

40. Truman and Leahy are quoted in Len Giovannitti and Fred Freed, *The Decision to Drop the Bomb* (New York: Coward, McCann, 1965), 320 and 323, respectively.

41. *Hiroshima* was also reprinted in Hersey's *Here to Stay: Studies in Human Tenacity* (1963), a collection of his essays.

Chapter Two

1. "The Mechanics of a Novel," *Yale University Library Gazette* 27, no. 1 (July 1952): 3.

2. "The Need for Memory," typescript of address to Baltimore Hebrew College, 1984. Quotations in the following paragraph are from this source.

3. Except as noted, quotations in the next six paragraphs are taken from "The Mechanics of a Novel."

4. The translators were identified in "The Need for Memory" as Mark Nowogrodsky (translating from Polish) and (from Yiddish) Lucy Davidowicz, later

the prominent Holocaust historian. They are pseudonymously mentioned in acknowledgments published in *The Wall*.

5. "The Need for Memory," 17–18.

6. Nancy Lyman Huse, *The Survival Tales of John Hersey* (Troy, N.Y.: Whitston, 1983), 76.

7. "The Novel of Contemporary History," *Atlantic Monthly,* November 1949, 80.

8. Girgus, "Against the Grain: The Achievement of John Hersey," 73.

9. "The Need for Memory."

10. David Daiches, "Review and Testament," *Commentary* 9 (April 1950): 385–88.

11. See Alred Kazin on such reviews in "John Hersey and Noach Levinson," *New Yorker,* 4 March 1950, 240–45.

12. "Our Far-Flung Correspondents. The Kibbutz," *New Yorker,* 19 April 1952, 89–99.

13. "The Novel of Contemporary History," 80.

Chapter Three

1. Interview with the author, 13 August 1987.

2. Throughout this book, Chinese place names are spelled as they appear in the work at hand.

3. "Alternatives to Apathy," *U.N. World* 1 (May 1947): 75–76.

4. "Peggety's Parcel of Shortcomings," *Atlantic Monthly,* June 1950, 30.

5. Samuel Girgus (131 ff.) links *The Marmot Drive* to Hawthorne's tales in a detailed discussion of Hersey's affinity with Hawthorne's ironic vision of "innocence incomplete without tragedy."

6. Ibid., 155.

7. "Experience by Battle," *Life,* 27 December 1943, 71.

8. Randall H. Waldron, "The Naked, the Dead, and the Machine: A New Look at Norman Mailer's First Novel," *PMLA* 87, no. 2 (March 1972): 271–77.

9. See the extended study of this situation in Robert N. Hudspeth, "A Definition of Modern Nihilism: Hersey's *The War Lover,*" *University Review* 35 (Summer 1969): 243–49.

10. Brad Leithauser, "Books: No Loyalty to DNA," *New Yorker,* 9 January 1989, 94–98 (review of *Mind Children: The Future of Robot and Human Intelligence,* by Hans Moravec).

11. Interview with the author, 13 August 1987.

12. Dee, "The Art of Fiction, XCII. John Hersey," 218.

13. "The Brilliant Jughead," *New Yorker,* 28 July 1945, 39. Reprinted in Hersey's collection *Life Sketches* (New York: Knopf, 1989).

14. "Why Do Students Bog Down on First R?" *Life,* 24 May 1954, 36–37.

15. "Intelligence, Choice, and Consent." Pamphlet published for the Woodrow Wilson Foundation, 1959, 12. Reprinted in part in *Life Sketches*.

16. Ibid., 23.

17. Ibid., 27–28.

18. Margaret Halsey, "The Shortest Way with Assenters"; B. F. Skinner, "May We Have a Positive Contribution?"; Carl F. Hansen, "Educator vs. Educationist"; Robert Gorham Davis, "Arrangement in Black and White"; and William Jay Smith, "The Truly Handicapped," *New Republic,* 10 October 1960, 21–25.

Chapter Four

1. "The Need for Memory," typescript of unpublished address to Baltimore Hebrew College, 1984, 10.

2. Interview with the author, 13 August 1987.

3. Ibid.

4. Dee, "The Art of Fiction, XCII. John Hersey," 216.

5. *Saturday Evening Post,* 26 September 1964, 34–43. Reprinted in *Life Sketches* (New York: Knopf, 1989).

6. His name is given in *Life Sketches,* 282.

7. Ralph Ellison, *Invisible Man* (New York: Random House, 1952), 439.

8. Webster Schott, untitled review of *White Lotus, New York Times Book Review,* 24 January 1965, 5; untitled review of *White Lotus, Times Literary Supplement,* 8 July 1965, 573.

9. Huse, *The Survival Tales of John Hersey,* 128.

10. Girgus, "Against the Grain: The Achievement of John Hersey," 171.

11. Interview with the author, 13 August 1987.

Chapter Five

1. For a firsthand account of the occasion, see Eric Goldman, *The Tragedy of Lyndon Johnson* (New York: Knopf, 1969), especially 455–67.

2. Dee, "The Art of Fiction, XCII. John Hersey," 240.

3. Interview with the author, 13 August 1987.

4. *The Writer's Craft* (New York: Knopf, 1974), 281; *Ralph Ellison: A Collection of Critical Essays* (Englewood Cliffs, N.J.: Prentice Hall, 1974), 18.

5. Interview with the author, 13 August 1987.

6. Oscar Handlin, "Reader's Choice," *Atlantic Monthly,* April 1966, 142.

7. Girgus, "Against the Grain: The Achievement of John Hersey," 227.

8. Interview with the author, 13 August 1987.

9. *The Writer's Craft,* 8.

10. Ibid., 9.

11. Interview with the author, 13 August 1987.

12. Hersey's observations in Mississippi that summer are detailed in "A Life for a Vote," *Saturday Evening Post,* 26 September 1974, 34–43. Reprinted in *Life Sketches* (New York: Knopf, 1989), 282–320.

13. Interview with the author, 13 August 1987.

14. Robert Conot, "One Night in Detroit," *New York Times Book Review,* 7 July 1968, 3.

15. Stephen Schlesinger, "Shoot-up in Detroit," *Atlantic Monthly,* September 1968, 124.

16. Nat Hentoff, "Waking Up White Folks Again," *New Republic,* 20 July 1968, 36.

17. "The Legend on the License," *Yale Review* 20, no. 1 (Autumn 1980): 14.

18. Interview with the author, 13 August 1987.

19. Ibid.

20. Ibid.

21. Whether as an officer in writers' organizations or as signatory to protests, Hersey has invariably been among American writers who have fought instances of censorship and proscription.

22. Interview with the author, 13 August 1987.

23. *The Writer's Craft,* 141.

24. Ibid., 145.

25. Ibid., 3.

26. Interview with the author, 13 August 1987.

27. Benjamin DeMott, untitled review of *Letter to the Alumni, New York Times Book Review,* 20 September 1970, 7.

28. Huse, *The Survival Tales of John Hersey,* 178–79.

Chapter Six

1. Some ideas in this chapter appear briefly in a different form in my review of the novel, "A Novel Explores the Character of a Missionary," Philadelphia *Inquirer,* 2 June 1985, sec. M, p. 1. I thank Carlin Romano, book editor of the *Inquirer,* for permission to adapt those ideas here.

2. "A Reporter at Large. Homecoming" (part 2, "A Posting to Tientsin"), *New Yorker,* 17 May 1982, 70.

3. John K. Fairbank, "Mission Impossible," *New York Review of Books,* 12 May 1985, 17.

4. Interview with the author, 13 August 1987.

5. Fairbank, "Mission Impossible," 17.

6. Kingsley Widmer, in *The Forties: Fiction, Poetry, and Drama,* ed. Warren French (Deland, Fla.: Everett Edwards, 1969), 143.

7. Karl, *American Fictions: 1920–1940,* 587.

Chapter Seven

1. Letter to the author, 21 December 1989.

2. "A Reporter at Large. Asymmetry," *New Yorker,* 7 September 1987, 36–53.

3. Izaak Walton, *The Compleat Angler* (New York: Modern Library, n.d. [text of the fourth edition, 1668]), 263

4. Elaine Kendall, "Hersey's *Fling* with Short Fiction," *Los Angeles Times,* 23 February 1990, E14–E15.

Chapter Eight

1. Introduction to *The Writer's Craft* (New York: Knopf, 1974), 3.

2. Samuel Girgus demonstrates this point eloquently and thoroughly in "Against the Grain: The Achievement of John Hersey."

Selected Bibliography

Primary Works

Books of Fiction

A Bell for Adano. New York: Knopf, 1944.
Blues. New York: Knopf, 1987. Imaginary conversations on fishing.
The Call. New York: Knopf, 1985.
The Child Buyer. New York: Knopf, 1960.
The Conspiracy. New York: Knopf, 1972.
Fling and Other Stories. New York: Knopf, 1990. Story collection.
The Marmot Drive. New York: Knopf, 1953.
My Petition for More Space. New York: Knopf, 1974.
A Single Pebble. New York: Knopf, 1956.
Too Far to Walk. New York: Knopf, 1966.
Under the Eye of the Storm. New York: Knopf, 1967.
The Wall. New York: Knopf, 1950.
The Walnut Door. New York: Knopf, 1977.
The War Lover. New York: Knopf, 1959.
White Lotus. New York: Knopf, 1965.

Books of Nonfiction

The Algiers Motel Incident. New York: Knopf, 1968.
Aspects of the Presidency. New Haven: Ticknor and Fields, 1980. Combines *The President* and 1951 *New Yorker* articles on President Harry S. Truman.
Here to Stay. New York: Knopf, 1963. Essay collection with reprinting of *Hiroshima*.
Hiroshima. New York: Knopf, 1946. Reprinting of *New Yorker* article.
Hiroshima: A New Edition with a Final Chapter Written Forty Years after the Explosion. New York: Knopf, 1985. Adds revision of *New Yorker* article, "Aftermath."
Into the Valley. New York: Knopf, 1943. Expanded, revised version of "The Battle of the River."
A Letter to the Alumni. New York: Knopf, 1970.
Life Sketches. New York: Knopf, 1989. Essays.
Men on Bataan. New York: Knopf, 1942.
The President. New York: Knopf, 1975. Revision of *New York Times Magazine* article on President Gerald R. Ford.

Edited Volumes

Ralph Ellison: A Collection of Critical Essays. Twentieth Century Views Series.
  Englewood Cliffs, N.J.: Prentice Hall, 1974.
The Writer's Craft. New York: Knopf, 1974. Anthology with commentary.

Short Stories

"Affinities." *Shenandoah* 37, no. 2 (1987): 3–21. Reprinted in *Fling and Other
  Stories.*
"The Announcement." *Atlantic Monthly,* October 1989, Reprinted in *Fling and
  Other Stories.*
"The Blouse." *Special Reports: Fiction,* May–July 1989, Reprinted in *Fling and
  Other Stories.*
"The Captain." *The Yacht,* November–December 1988, Reprinted in *Fling and
  Other Stories.*
"The Death of Buchan Walsh." *Atlantic Monthly,* April 1946, 80–86.
"A Fable South of Cancer." *47–the Magazine of the Year,* April 1947, 113–41.
"Fling." *Grand Street,* Summer 1987. Reprinted in *Fling and Other Stories.*
"God's Typhoon." *Atlantic Monthly,* June 1987, 72–78. Reprinted in *Fling and
  Other Stories.*
"Mr. Quintillian." *Yale Review* 77 (Autumn 1987): 1–24. Reprinted in *Fling and
  Other Stories.*
"Peggety's Parcels of Shortcomings." *Atlantic Monthly,* June 1950, 26–30. Re-
  printed in *Fling and Other Stories.*
"The Pen." *Atlantic Monthly,* June 1946, 84–87.
"Requiescat." *Paris Review* 30 (Summer 1988): 98–115. Reprinted in *Fling and
  Other Stories.*
"A Short Wait." *New Yorker,* 14 June 1947, 27–29.
"The Terrorist." *Esquire,* August 1987, 114–15. Reprinted in *Fling and Other
  Stories.*
"Why Were You Sent Out Here?" *Atlantic Monthly,* February 1947, 88–91. Re-
  printed in *Fling and Other Stories.*

Articles and Essays

"Alternatives to Apathy." *U.N. World* 1 (May 1947), 20–21, 70–76. On an every-
  day political philosophy.
"AMGOT at Work." *Life,* 23 August 1943, 29–31. Partial background for *A Bell
  for Adano.*
"The Battle of the River." *Life,* 23 November 1942, 99–116. Revised, expanded for
  Into the Valley.
"Better Classrooms for Less Money." *Saturday Review,* 12 September 1953, 18–19.
"The Brilliant Jughead." *New Yorker,* 28 July 1954, 25–39. On U.S. Army's cam-
  paign against illiteracy. Reprinted in *Life Sketches.*

"A Critic at Large. Agee." *New Yorker,* 18 July 1988 72–82. Searching as both criti-
    cism and reminiscence, especially of *Let Us Now Praise Famous Men* as a "classic
    work of metajournalism." Reprinted with minor changes as the introduction to
    a new edition of *Let Us Now Praise Famous Men.*

"Days, Nights, and a Few Years." *New Yorker,* 3 November 1945, 90–96. Review of
    Days and Nights, by Konstantin Simonov.

"Dialogue on Gorki Street." *Fortune,* January 1945, 149–51. Imaginary conversa-
    tion with fictitious Russian writer.

"Engineers of the Soul." *Time,* 9 October 1944, 99–102. On Soviet writers in
    wartime.

"Experience by Battle." *Life,* 27 December 1943, 48–84. Text accompanying re-
    productions of paintings by *Life* staff artists.

"First Job." *Yale Review* 76, no. 2 (Winter 1987): 183–97. Hersey as Sinclair
    Lewis's secretary. See "My Summer Job with Sinclair Lewis." Reprinted in *Life
    Sketches.*

"Friends of Public Education Rallied: Too Late." In *Freedom and Public Education,*
    edited by Ernest O. Melby and Morton Puner; 144–48. New York: Praeger,
    1953. Review of *This Happened in Pasadena,* by David Hulbird. On firing of
    school superintendent.

"Henry Luce's China Dream." *New Republic,* 2 May 1983, 27–32. See MacKinnon.
    Reprinted in *Life Sketches.*

"The Hills of Nicosia." *Time,* 9 August 1943, 30. Cabled report on Sicilian
    landings.

"Home to Warsaw." *Life,* 9 April 1945, 16–20. On Polish officer's return to ruins of
    his neighborhood.

"Intelligence, Choice, and Consent." Pamphlet published for the Woodrow Wilson
    Foundation, New York, 1959. Reprinted in part in *Life Sketches.*

"Introduction." In *Let Us Now Praise Famous Men,* by James Agee. Boston:
    Houghton Mifflin, 1988. New edition. Revision of "A Critic at Large. Agee."
    Reprinted in *Life Sketches.*

"Joe Grew, Ambassador to Japan." *Life,* 15 July 1940, 76–83. Hersey's first byline.

"Joe Is Home Now." *Life,* 3 July 1944, 66–80. On returning veterans. Reprinted,
    revised, in *Here to Stay.*

"Kamikaze." *Life,* 30 July 1945, 68–75. Action in battle of Okinawa.

"The Legend on the License." *Yale Review* 20, no. 1 (Autumn 1980): 1–25. On dis-
    tinctions between fiction and journalism with reference to Capote, Mailer, and
    Tom Wolfe.

"Letter from Chungking." *New Yorker,* 16 March 1946, 80–87. On departure of
    Generalissimo and Madame Chiang from wartime capital.

"Letter from Peiping." *New Yorker,* 4 May 1946, 86–96. On political situation. "No
    matter what the United States does, I am afraid, China is in for a long, sharp,
    bloody struggle."

"Letter from Shanghai." *New Yorker,* 9 February 1946, 82–90. American service-men on liberty in China's largest and most cosmopolitan city.

"A Life for a Vote." *Saturday Evening Post,* 26 September 1964, 34–43. Voter regis-tration in Mississippi. Reprinted in *Life Sketches.*

"Lillian Hellman." *New Republic,* 18 September 1976, 25–27. Tribute on occasion of Hellman's receiving the MacDowell Prize. Reprinted in *Life Sketches.*

"Marine in China." *Life,* 27 May 1946, 17–24.

"The Marines on Guadalcanal." *Life,* 9 November 1942, 36–39.

"The Mechanics of a Novel." *Yale University Library Gazette* 27 (July 1952): 1–11. Address on receiving Howland Memorial Prize and depositing first draft of *The Wall* in the Yale University Library.

"A Mistake of Terrifically Horrible Proportions." In *Manzanar,* by John Armor and Peter Wright, 3–66. Commentary by John Hersey. Photographs by Ansel Adams. New York: Times Books, 1988. On World War II relocation of Japa-nese Americans.

"Mr. President." *New Yorker,* 7 April 1951, 42–56; 14 April, 1951, 38–53; 21 April 1951, 36–57; 28 April 1951, 36–52; 5 May 1951, 36–53. On Presi-dent Harry S. Truman. Reprinted, revised, in *Aspects of the Presidency.* 14 April segment reprinted in *Life Sketches.*

"Mr. Secretary Marshall." *Collier's,* 29 March 1947, 11–13; 5 April 1947, 18–19; 12 April 1947, 78–81. On Secretary of State George C. Marshall.

"My Summer Job with Sinclair Lewis." *New York Times Book Review,* 10 May 1987, 26–38. Expanded version appeared as "First Job," *Yale Review* 76, no. 2 (Winter 1987): 183–97. "First Job" reprinted in *Life Sketches.*

"Nine Men on a Four Man Raft." *Life,* 2 November 1942, 54–57. Interview of sur-vivors of B-17 crew from Tokyo raid aboard USS *Hornet.*

"1968: The Year of the Triphammer." *Syracuse Herald-American,* 26 November 1978. Sixteen-page tabloid supplement distributed to numerous American newspapers. Summary, interpretation of events.

"The Novel of Contemporary History." *Atlantic Monthly,* November 1949, 80–84. On distinctions between fiction and journalism.

"Our Far-Flung Correspondents. The Kibbutz." *New Yorker,* 19 April 1952, 89–99. On the kibbutz as an example of "the mutability of socialism."

"Prisoner 339, Klooga." *Life,* 30 October 1944, 72–83. Interview with man who had just escaped last German efforts at genocide in the Baltic states. Reprinted in *Here to Stay* and *Life Sketches.*

"Profile. The Happy, Happy Beggar." *New Yorker,* 11 May 1946, 34–47. On Father Walter P. Morse and his mission in Ichang, China. Reprinted in *Life Sketches.*

"Profile. The Old Man." *New Yorker,* 3 January 1947, 28–37; 10 January 1948, 30–40; 17 January 1948, 30–41. On Bernard Baruch. 3 January segment re-printed in *Life Sketches.*

"PT Squadron in the South Pacific." *Life,* 10 May 1943, 74–87. "Three skippers tell how they fought Jap warships."

"Red Pepper Village." *Life,* 26 August 1946, 92–105. Communal life in Chinese country village.

"A Reporter at Large. Assymetry." *New Yorker,* 7 September 1987, 36–53. Report on Moscow meeting of International Physicians for the Prevention of Nuclear War.

"A Reporter at Large. The Communization of Crow Village." *New Yorker,* 27 July 1946, 38–47. Account of Chinese village life with generalizations on Chinese communism.

"A Reporter at Large. Hiroshima." *New Yorker,* 31 August 1946, 15–68. Original publication of account of six survivors of first atom bomb.

"A Reporter at Large. Hiroshima: The Aftermath." *New Yorker,* 15 July 1985, 37–63. Later lives of the six survivors. Reprinted, revised, in 1985 edition of *Hiroshima.*

"A Reporter at Large. Homecoming." *New Yorker,* 10 May 1982, 49–79; 17 May 1982, 46–70; 24 May 1982, 44–66; 31 May 1982, 47–67. On Hersey's first visit to Tientsin since 1946.

"A Reporter at Large. The Ingathering of Exiles." *New Yorker,* 24 November 1951, 92–113. On Israeli immigration problems.

"A Reporter at Large. Journey toward a Sense of Being Treated Well." *New Yorker,* 2 March 1957, 39–87. Odyssey of a Hungarian refugee family from Budapest to Austrian relocation camp. Reprinted in *Here to Stay.*

"A Reporter at Large. Long Haul with Variables." *New Yorker,* 8 September 1945, 44–57. Return of the Eighty-sixth Division, U.S. Army, to the United States.

"A Reporter at Large. Over the Mad River." *New Yorker,* 17 September 1955, 118–40. Rescue operations during Hurricane Diana. Reprinted in *Here to Stay* and *Life Sketches.*

"A Reporter at Large. Successors." *New Yorker,* 16 December 1974, 46–82. Interviews in Israel of Holocaust survivors and families. Reprinted in *Here to Stay* and *Life Sketches.*

"A Reporter in China. Two Weeks' Water Away." *New Yorker,* 18 May 1946, 59–69; 25 May 1946, 54–69. Account of transporting Nationalist troops on American LSTs.

"A Reporter in Shanghai." *New Yorker,* 23 March 1946, 32–36. Account of Western businessman trying to start up again.

"Ricksha No. 34." *Life,* 3 June 1946, 63–70. Account of Beijing ricksha driver as example of China's strengths and weaknesses.

"Russia Likes Plays Too." *Time,* 23 October 1944, 48–50. Prospects for Moscow's theater compared favorably with New York's.

"A Short Talk with Erlanger." *Life,* 29 October 1945, 108–22. On U.S. Army's use of narcosynthesis. Reprinted in *Here to Stay.*

"Survival." *New Yorker,* 17 June 1944, 31–34. Account of Lt. John F. Kennedy and PT-109. Reprinted in *Here to Stay* and *Life Sketches.*

"Talk with John Cheever." *New York Times Book Review,* 6 March 1977, 1, 24–27. Interview accompanying Joan Didion's review of *Falconer.*

"Test of Heart and Mind." *Life,* 4 September 1964, 62–64. On voting in Mississippi.

"The Triumph of Numbers." *Atlantic Monthly,* October 1980, 78–87. Revision of address on the humanities and sciences in higher education.

"The Wayward Press. Conference in Room 474." *New Yorker,* 16 December, 1950, 78–90. News briefing during the Korean War. Reprinted, revised, in *Aspects of the Presidency.*

"Why Do Students Bog Down on First R?" *Life,* 24 May 1954, 136–50.

"Why Were You Sent Out Here?" *Atlantic Monthly,* February 1947, 88–91. Story.

"Yale '36—Look at Them Now," *Harper's,* September 1952, 21–28. Brief survey, briefer reminiscence.

Unpublished Material

"The Need for Memory." Typescript of address upon receiving the Stiller Prize, Baltimore Hebrew College, 1984.

Secondary Works

Bibliography

Huse, Nancy Lyman. *John Hersey and James Agee: A Reference Guide,* 7–54. Boston: G. K. Hall, 1978. Contains selective, annotated secondary bibliography, organized chronologically, 1942–77.

Books

Girgus, Samuel B. "Against the Grain: The Achievement of John Hersey." Ph.D. dissertation, University of New Mexico, 1972. Study of ideas in Hersey's writings through *The Conspiracy* in context of contemporary thought and literary influences.

Huse, Nancy Lyman. "John Hersey: The Writer and His Times." Ph.D. dissertation, University of Chicago, 1975.

————.*The Survival Tales of John Hersey.* Troy, N.Y.: Whitston, 1983. Critical study of Hersey's fiction and journalism through 1977—broader and more inclusive than the title suggests.

Articles and Parts of Books

Burton, Arthur. "Existential Conceptions in John Hersey's Novel 'The Child Buyer.' " *Journal of Existential Psychology* 2 (Fall 1961):243–58.

Daiches, David. "Record and Statement." *Commentary* 9 (April 1950):385–88. Review of *The Wall*.

Dee, Jonathan. "The Art of Fiction XCII. John Hersey." *Paris Review* 100 (Summer/Fall 1986):211–49. Interview ranging over background before Hiroshima and at Pierson College, *The Wall*, *The Call*, opinions on fiction and reporting.

Fairbank, John K. "Mission Impossible." *New York Review of Books*, 10 May 1985, 17–18. Review of *The Call* by noted sinologist.

Fiedler, Leslie. "The Novel in the Post-Political World." *Partisan Review* 23 (Summer 1956):358–65. Comment on *A Single Pebble*, among other novels.

Fishkin, Shelley Fisher. *From Fact to Fiction: Journalism and Imaginative Writing in America*. Baltimore: Johns Hopkins University Press, 1985. See index. Cites "Legend on the License" and Hersey's differences with Norman Mailer on journalism and fiction.

Geismar, Maxwell. "John Hersey: The Revival of Conscience." In his *American Moderns: From Rebellion to Conformity*, 180–86. New York: Hill and Wang, 1958. Adapted from earlier review of *The Wall*, essay on Hersey as a social novelist.

Guilfoil, Kelsey. "John Hersey: Fact and Fiction." *English Journal* 39 (September 1950):355–60. Early consideration of whether Hersey is a journalist or a novelist.

Haltresht, Michael. "Dreams, Visions, and Myths in John Hersey's *White Lotus*." *Western Georgia College Review* 6 (May 1973):24–28.

Hudspeth, Robert N. "A Definition of Modern Nihilism: Hersey's *The War Lover*." *University Review* 35 (Summer 1969):243–49. Study of the novel as a conflict between Marrow's nihilism and Boman's growing humanism.

Kazin, Alfred. "John Hersey and Noach Levinson." *New Yorker*, 4 March 1950, 96–100. Review of *The Wall*.

McDonnell, Thomas P. "Hersey's Allegorical Novels." *Catholic World* 95 (July 1962):240–45.

MacKinnon, Stephen R., and Oris Friesen. *China Reporting: An Oral History of American Journalism in the 1930s and 1940s*. Berkeley: University of California Press, 1987. Contains Hersey's address to a 1982 conference organized by the editors (see "Henry Luce's China Dream") and his comparison of the difficulty of wartime reporting from China versus that in the Soviet Union.

Moses, Robert. "Informal Notes Taken on Reading John Hersey on Yale." *National Review*, 7 February 1971, 142–44. Review of *A Letter to the Alumni* by alumnus and noted planner.

Sanders, David. "John Hersey: War Correspondent into Novelist." In *New Voices in American Studies*, edited by Ray B. Browne, 49–58. Lafayette, Ind.: Purdue University Press, 1966. Compares influences of Hersey's wartime background on *A Bell for Adano* and *The Wall*.

Schorer, Mark. *Sinclair Lewis: An American Life*. New York: McGraw-Hill, 1961. See index. Describes Hersey's summer job with Lewis in 1937.

Spain, Tom. "PW Interviews: John Hersey." *Publishers Weekly*, 10 May 1985, 232–33. Interview emphasizing *The Call*.

Swanberg, W. A. *Luce and His Empire*, 148–49, 189. New York: Scribner, 1972. Details of Hersey's employment with *Time* and *Life*.

Waldmeir, Joseph. *American Novels of the Second World War*, 30–33. The Hague: Mouton, 1969. Comment on *A Bell for Adano* and *The War Lover*.

Waldron, Randall H. "The Naked, the Dead, and the Machine: A New Look at Norman Mailer's First Novel." *PMLA* 87, no. 2 (March 1972):271–77. References to conflicts between machines and human beings in *A Bell for Adano* and *The War Lover*.

Walsh, Jeffrey. *American War Literature: 1914 to Vietnam*, 136–37, 149–51. New York: St. Martin's, 1982. Comments on *A Bell for Adano* and *The Wall*.

Weber, Ronald. *The Literature of Fact: Literary Non-Fiction in American Writing*, 66–72. Athens: Ohio University Press, 1980. Analysis of Hersey's reporting technique in *Hiroshima* and *The Algiers Motel Incident*.

White, Theodore. *In Search of History: A Personal Narrative*. New York: Harper and Row, 1978. Reminiscence of meeting Hersey in Chungking.

Yavenditti, Michael J. "John Hersey and the American Conscience: The Reception of *Hiroshima*." *Pacific Historical Review* 43 (February 1974):24–49. Study of public reception of *Hiroshima* and the book's influence on peace movements.

Zavarzadeh, Mas'ud. *The Mythopoeic Reality: The Postwar American Nonfiction Novel*, 94–102. Urbana: University of Illinois Press, 1976. Analysis of *Hiroshima* as "exegetical nonfiction novel."

Index